NOTES FR(

My goodness, it's been 22 years since I've been receiving your writings under the title French Word-A-Day! How time flies! I just wanted to share with you all the pleasure I've had in reading you regularly. It has brought me closer to the south of France that I adore and has softened homesickness. Thank you for your prose. I have loved it all these years.

— *Martine Baboin*

I just realized that what I really enjoy about your blog has very little to do with French, although that is why I thought it was the reason I've been reading it for years. Your ability to share your emotional life is very special and makes me (and I suspect, all of us), feel connected to you, your family and your grand adventure in France. Thank you!

— *Ron Cann*

Your journal is a lovely combination of everyday family happenings with many useful phrases and new words to learn. It is well written, and I look forward to reading it on Thursdays.

— *Joan Souder*

I love your posts. Reading them…is like spending a bit of time in France without the hassle of airports, money changing, etc. You always transmit the essence of an experience, if you will. I taste what you're tasting, smell what you're smelling, and seem to absorb La Belle France through my pores. I cannot imagine ever unsubscribing. Please keep it up!"

— *Anna Johnston*

Your stories in my inbox are a treat. They are a time to sit back and travel to France in the form of a creative glimpse into life in another place close to my heart.

— *Kerry Leglu*

While I look forward to, and enjoy, your beautiful posts on Instagram, it is your blog that has made me feel as if I'm in your circle of friends. This is invaluable in today's fast paced and trendy content. Stay true to you, dear friend!

— *Stacy Lund*

Your weekly reports from France are a ray of sunshine, even when you share stories of challenging times. I'm very grateful for your generous spirit in letting us in on your family's adventures. You are a gifted observer, and photographer.

— *Ann Borman*

You write a brilliant blog and you reach out to so many with your kindness, humor and generous spirit. In a busy world, you encourage us to stop and think and to count our blessings. Your family life is rarely smooth, but your courage and honesty lead the way. You are the best kind of teacher. You never stop learning. You inspire us to do the same. And what will remain of us is love.

— *Jeanne Goulding*

FWAD is a wonderful site. It has definitely helped me keep up with French in the 50+ years since I completed my French major in college, and has acquainted me with slang and many useful words and phrases. It has familiarized me with the French culture I mostly missed by not living for long in France.

— *Marianne Rankin*

Your personal anecdotes beautifully illustrate the warmth and joy of being reunited with loved ones.

— *Aurelio Johnson*

A Y.EAR

in a

FRENCH LIFE

VOLUME ONE

Kristin Espinasse

FWD

Provence, France

OTHER BOOKS BY KRISTIN ESPINASSE

Words in a French Life

Blossoming in Provence

First French "Essais"

The Lost Gardens:
A Story of Two Vineyards and a Marriage

A YEAR IN A FRENCH LIFE

FWD books may be purchased in bulk at special discounts for sales
promotion, corporate gifts, ministry, fund-raising, or educational purposes.
Special editions can also be created to specifications.
For details, contact kristin.espinasse@gmail.com.

Cover and interior design by *TLCBookDesign.com*.
Cover by Monica Thomas; Interior by Erin Stark

Translation by Kristin Espinasse; translation edits by Kristin Espinasse

Paperback ISBN: 978-2-9598993-0-0 | ebook ISBN: 978-2-9598993-1-7

Legal deposit: February 2025
FWD, La Ciotat, France

For Heidi

NOTE TO
MY READERS

As you journey through these stories, you'll notice a section at the end of each chapter called FRENCH VOCABULARY. This glossary is here to help you enjoy the flavor of the French words and expressions that weave through my writing. Whether you're a seasoned Francophile or just beginning to explore the language, I hope these bits of vocabulary enhance your reading experience, offering a deeper connection to the cultural nuances and everyday moments of life in France.

Rather than focusing on perfecting your French, I encourage you to embrace the spirit of discovery, much like I did when I first arrived in France. Language, like life, is a process of learning and adapting, and I hope these glossaries bring a sense of ease and curiosity as you read along.

Bon voyage,

Kristi

PROLOGUE

*S*ince fulfilling my dream of moving to France, my mom has been present at every milestone. Though an ocean away in Mexico, some thirty years ago Jules packed a tuxedo, braving the friendly skies to walk me down the aisle at a cathedral in Marseille. She left Yelapa for the birth of our son Max in Marseille and, two years later, for daughter Jackie's *naissance* in Aix-en-Provence. When we moved to the vineyard, Mom touched down near Sainte Cécile-les-Vignes for *la vendange*, in time to cheer the harvesters with her charm and charisma. A gypsy at heart, Jules dreamed of retiring to a treehouse on the hill above the *oliviers* when we moved to Saint Cyr-sur-Mer. No *EPHAD* in her future! I used to shake my head at Mom's outlandish ideas, *une cabane dans les arbres, vraiment*!

When Mom became *une veuve* and was left on her own in Puerto Vallarta, it was a turning point in our lives. Over the phone, my sister in Denver and I discussed options: Heidi had a renovated basement, and I had a converted garage. Was either suitable? Meanwhile, Jules had already found a solution. "I'm moving to the jungle!" our outlander declared, echoing a longtime dream of leaving her apartment at the marina for the lush hinterland. Her housekeeper's brother had a rental—a tin-roofed structure along a crowded dirt lane dotted with pigs, chickens, and *poubelles*. Heidi and I were dubious, but

Mom insisted she'd have a village watching over her. She eagerly moved to her paradise, finding joy in sweeping up the neighborhood, a band of local children ever in tow.

Thousands of miles from Mexico, Heidi and I were going through similar transitions: my sister's lease was up and my husband and I had abandoned our second vineyard for a small bungalow. Just when we were settled, Mom was robbed at home!

Heidi immediately flew in and escorted her out of Paradise Lost. Mom's life savings were stuffed into envelopes and taped inside their blouses before mother and daughter cleared customs, reorganized in Denver, and Mom bravely flew on to France, her worldly possessions (including both tropical monkey lamps, a marble chest, and a candelabra) in three *valises*.

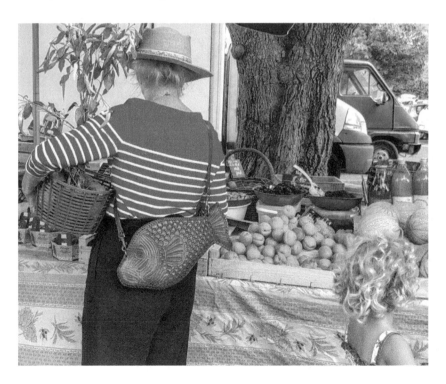

We added a kitchen and bath to our glorified garage before Jules moved in with our lovable golden retriever, Smokey, to imagine her future: stay? move to Spain? return to the Arizona desert where she raised us? Our "artist-in-residence" needed little, though she yearned for a scooter–an idea we vetoed until it became clear even to Mom that she was slowing down.

In the seven years since she immigrated, Mom hasn't learned French but navigates this foreign life using the language of her heart. It's the same language my children, my husband, and I practice as we accompany Mom through this *stage de la vie*, figuring out long-term care options for our free-spirited elder. Jules still wants a treehouse. *Et pourquoi pas?* These are her golden years in France, the land where dreams come true.

FRENCH VOCABULARY

la naissance
birth

la vendange
grape harvest

l'olivier
olive tree

l'EHPAD
nursing home

la cabane dans les arbres
treehouse

vraiment
really

la veuve
widow

la poubelle
garbage

la valise
suitcase

la stage de la vie
stage of life

et pourquoi pas
and why not?

INTRODUCTION

*J*ust as my mom has been a constant presence during life's most significant moments, writing has been my way of capturing the fleeting experiences of living in France. It has also helped me find meaning in the personal struggles of adapting to a foreign country and navigating life's many challenges.

For years, I've tried to gather these blog stories into a book—ever since my last compilation was published a decade ago. You'd think it would be simple to pull together a few dozen blog entries, paste them into a manuscript, and—abracadabra—upload them to a print-on-demand service. After all, there are so many tools and support systems available for indie publishers. But, after struggle upon struggle—*après avoir bien galéré*—I realized I couldn't do this alone.

Back in 2003, as a newly-minted blogger, I managed to put these early *billets* into a manuscript, design a cover, and send the files off to "Instant Publisher" in the States. They printed the books and shipped them, 500 at a time, to me in France. In turn, I shipped them one by one and sometimes three by three (many of you graciously bought all three volumes) to readers worldwide. These little awkward editions (one was missing part of the title on its spine, and all three lacked proper interior formatting) were selling like hotcakes, and I was finally making a living as a writer—or

at least helping to supplement my husband's income. I was now a stay-at-home mom *with a vocation!* My publishing gig might have continued even today if it weren't for an unexpected email from a "Big Five" *éditeur…*

It was a dream come true when Simon & Schuster professionally edited my essays into a hardbound book: *Words in a French Life.* While the memoir did well, selling over 50,000 copies, it wasn't enough for the publisher to want to pursue a Volume 2. When my editor suggested fiction, I froze, having only ever written short essays. Allowing all my insecurities to come out and feast, I let my contract with a New York agent run out and I returned to what was "easiest" or most familiar to me: blogging. I made a few half-hearted attempts at printing more books but had lost my self-publishing mojo.

Several years later, a reader reached out, and I had the chance to work with Tami and Erin at TLC Book Design. It was exciting to see two more books published in 2009 and 2014! But after our *déménagement* from the vineyard, I floundered for a while. Then, in the beginning of 2024, fueled by the positive comments on the blog, the dream was rekindled. I realized part of the difficulty in gathering the stories was the overwhelming scope of it all: there were 22 years of archives to sort through! Finally, the thought came: *Begin where you are.* Just do your best with your current stories and enter them into the manuscript, one by one.

This decision helped me focus on the story at hand and stick to a narrative. As I worked, the title for the book surfaced naturally:

A YEAR IN A FRENCH LIFE

Finally, this title sounded right, given that the book is based on this blog "A Day in a French Life." With these pieces of the puzzle

in place, I was off and running! Well, until the formatting woes, cover conundrums, etc., drained me, and the doubts returned. *A quoi bon?* Why bother making a book when it's so much easier to just keep blogging? As long as I kept mumbling "*A quoi bon?*" I was stuck.

Just when I was considering giving up, my sister Heidi called. She assured me it would all come together. "Keep at it!"

I was soon back at my manuscript, and things were looking clearer. This overwhelming project felt *faisable*. Around this time, I received several book cover options from TLC Book Designs, whom I'm pleased to be working with again. *A Year in the French Life* will be published in 2025 with the help of faith, friends, and family. While I may like to do things on my own, experience is showing me that life is better together. *La vie est mieux ensemble.*

FRENCH VOCABULARY

galérer
to struggle, have trouble

après avoir bien galéré
after struggle upon struggle

un billet
blog post

un éditeur
publisher

le déménagement
move

à quoi bon?
Why bother?

cela aussi passera
this too shall pass

faisable
feasible

JANUARY

Janvier

1

BONNE ANNÉE

"*Bonne Année! Meilleurs Vœux! Surtout la bonne santé!*" Entering our local *supérette* for some fresh milk and eggs, I see the shopkeepers huddled around *la caisse*, bright smiles on their faces as they deliver cheery New Year's greetings. This jolly outpouring reminds me of one more blessing in the new year: all the familiar faces of our neighborhood and all of the local *commerces* that we sometimes take for granted.

We learned our local fishmongers have finally gone out of business and what a great loss to our *quartier*.

"*C'est dommage*," I say to Jean-Marc. "After all that work, I hope the couple are following their dream to retire in Spain!"

"Do you want to open *une poissonnerie?*" Jean-Marc teases me.

"*Mais bien sur que non! C'est juste que….*" It's just that I'm sad they are gone, and I regret not visiting them more often. *Poissonnerie Chez Laure*, we hear, will be replaced by *une rôtisserie* and, as much as we love roast chicken, *dans les parages* there are now four *commerces de volailles rôties….*

…et plus de poisson!

Tant pis! We cannot begin 2024 with regrets. Better to start the year with *les bonnes intentions.* So, on New Year's Day, towards the end of our morning walk, I invited Jean-Marc for coffee and a croissant at Plaza Beach. Daily, we pass by this café along the seafront and wave *bonjour* to Matthieu, *le patron,* but we never stop to order anything. (We did give Matthieu some business when my sister, Heidi, was here, last summer, when our *smala*—including Jules—gathered there several times for *l'apéro.* I have happy memories of my niece and nephew, and Matthieu regaling us with an elaborate cheese platter.)

If one New Year's Goal is to give our locals more business, another is to let them know they are appreciated. *"Bonne Année!"* I greeted Matthieu as we sat down with our dog. "We don't come here often enough but I wanted you to know that what you are doing is *impressionnant*! (Indeed, from a little hole in the wall, Matthieu has created an extended terrace café. He must cross the busy boulevard dozens of times each day to reach it from his tiny *local* beside the surf shop.) "We see you working so hard every day. Do you ever sit down?"

As awkward as the delivery might have been, my words were rewarded with a warm smile and an avowal: *"Si je m'assois je ne pourrai pas me relever. If I sit down, I won't be able to get back up!"* And like that, our barista was off to cross the busy road once again and fire up the espresso machine.

Moments later Matthieu returned with some fresh water for Ricci. Despite all the tables he was tending, he paused to bring our dog a refreshment!

That bowl of *eau fraîche*, delivered as it was, unexpectedly, in an empty ice cream carton, struck a few chords inside of me. As over-sentimental as it sounds, it touched my heartstrings. It was a small detail, the little water trough, but it was meaningful.

Out over the waterfront, sun rays dazzled the surface of the sea. Meantime, the little water trough held its own sparkle, which skipped across the water's surface, like one kindness pursuing another: our own and that of the receiver-turned-giver. An endless cycle of goodwill, born simply of intention.

FRENCH VOCABULARY

Bonne Année
Happy New Year

Meilleurs Vœux
Season's Greetings

la bonne santé
good health

la supérette
convenience store

la caisse
cash register

le commerce
business

le quartier
neighborhood

c'est dommage
it's too bad

la poissonnerie
fish shop

**mais bien
sûr que non**
of course not

c'est juste que
it's just that

la rôtisserie
rotisserie

dans les parages
in the vicinity

**le commerce
de volailles rôties**
roast poultry
business

plus de poisson
no more fish

tant pis
oh well

**les bonnes
intentions**
good intentions

**le patron
(la patronne)**
the owner

impressionnante
impressive

la smala
large family

l'apéro (m)
pre-dinner drink

le local
unit, space, room

**si je m'assois
je ne pourrai pas
me relever**
if I sit down
I won't be able
to get back up

l'eau fraîche (f)
fresh water

2

S'ENFUIR

After Jean-Marc left for Le Beausset Saturday, to help a friend plant grapevines, Ricci and I strolled to our neighborhood *marché paysan*, to buy fruits and vegetables. I'm going to take it easy today. Make a hearty lunch, and relax this morning, I thought to myself, already feeling peaceful. In the parking lot where our farmer's market pops up weekly, I struggled with a few baskets of produce while managing my dog. I decided to briefly attach Ricci to one of the fold-out tables, where all the produce baskets were resting. Beneath a giant plane tree, I was chatting with a vendor when *un bruit soudain* startled my dog...

The noise sent Ricci fleeing from the table. The clasp of her harness having snapped, Ricci took off like a bullet! I watched in horror, feeling like the one who had pulled the trigger. How could I have taken that risk! Why hadn't I tied her more carefully! I dropped my *panier* and shot out of the municipal parking lot.

Ricci careened toward traffic, her leash bobbing along the narrow *trottoir*, pursued by frantic me. I heard the cars in the roundabout screech to a halt as our frightened dog cleared the two-lane road in front of La Pharmacie Saint Jean. (Oh, Saint Jean—patron saint of shepherds—where were you when my little *berger* ran off?)

Shooting down the sidewalk, cars passing her closely on her left, the fugitive startled a few walkers who did a double-take when next they saw me flying by. *"Ma chienne! Ma chienne!"* Two hairdressers enjoying *une clope* in front of the *salon de coiffure* locked eyes with me as I darted past. I could feel their concern and picked up my step. Adrenaline coursing through my veins, I saw every detail, even though my eyes were fixed on *le champ de vision* into which my spooked dog had vanished.

Clipping past the surf shop, *la fleuriste*, and the *boulangerie* that just went out of business…I charged after my little dog, clunk-clunk-clunk in my daughter's riding boots, one size too big. Barely slowing to look both ways, I shot across two lanes to reach the promenade and kept running when my legs began to slow. Things were looking bleak.

RICCI! RICCI! RICCI! my shouting turned to muffled please… *oh please! oh please! oh please! …God please!* With Ricci out of sight, my words were more a mantra than a calling, a means to tame the terror I felt inside, to drown out other words that told me my dog might soon be crushed by a car.

I passed several walkers who, unaware of the drama unfolding, saw only a deranged woman babbling in bad French. *"Ma chienne s'est échappée! Ma chienne s'est échappée!"*

I ran a few blocks further and…there she was! Down on the beach. My heart filled with hope. This is the usual spot where we play drop and run (I drop down at a distance and Ricci charges across the beach into my arms). But just when it looked like this nightmare was over, Ricci, panicked and fled.

"Attrapez ma chienne! Attrapez ma chienne s'il vous plaît!" I thundered from the sidewalk, but a dozen swimmers preparing to brave the cold January waters did not understand the deranged foreigner shouting from the boardwalk.

Ricci shot up to the *digue*, disappearing yet again. I had missed my chance. *Oh God I missed my chance!* Would it be the only one? She was now headed to the busy roundabout where traffic picks up. "Ricci!" I cried in vain.

My mind reeled. *Why is she running away from me—her big sheep?* In the 3 months since we brought her home from the farm, she's herded me like *une brebis*. More than a little shepherd, Ricci is a Velcro dog, a veritable *pot de colle*. She is my complete shadow. I know she was spooked but why was she still running away from me? Did she feel she could no longer trust me? Did she, when I tied her to that table and next she heard *POP*, mistake it for an attack?

"Vous avez vu ma chienne? Ma chienne!" I shouted to anyone listening. "She went that way, past the telephone booth," a man said, but my gut told me he was mistaken. Another man arrived in time to point me straight ahead. Arriving at the one-mile marker in this unexpected sprint, gathering what force remained in my 56-year-old legs, I took off again, with a new mantra gurgling out of me:

JESUS, I BEG YOU! JESUS, I BEG YOU! I didn't care if I sounded like a mad-dashing religious fanatic. Or that faith is something you keep to yourself. Nothing mattered anymore except a miracle, an intervention, the hand of God in this impossible matter.

Just when all hope was lost, the man from the vegetable stand sped past me on his electric *trottinette*. I thought he had dropped out of the race a while back, but no! Here he was and I knew, I just knew, he would find her. He spotted her another block ahead and managed, along with a few others to corral her back around until, HOLY MOLY!, she was now running to me!

In case my little fugitive was still under the spell of panic that set her rocketing across the bay, I dropped, threw my arms out as wide as they could stretch, and grabbed her as she ran up. Whether a miracle of miracles, or a simple answered prayer, my sweet, scared dog was guided safely back to me. Oh, Ricci!

Thanks to all who helped along the way: to the jogger who immediately sped up, to the merchant who dropped his vegetable cart and hopped on his *trottinette*, to the walkers I could barely see in the far-off distance who reached for my dog. THANK YOU! And if you are a *Ciotaden*, a local, and you saw a madly wild woman screaming "REE-CHEE! GOD HELP ME!" you now know this saga had a happy ending. The moral of the story is: no matter how cautious we are with our animals, when their innate instinct for survival kicks in, they are out of our control. The best we can do is count on the goodwill of others, who care and who take the time to help. *Merci! Merci beaucoup!* Even if I did not get a chance to thank you—dear jogger, dear walkers—I saw you and you are everything! Finally, please visit the farmers market in the St. Jean quarter, open weekends. Adrien, the owner's son, now runs it. But he and his colleague, Geoffrey, dropped everything this morning to help us!

FRENCH VOCABULARY

s'enfuir
to flee, escape

Le Beausset
town near Bandol

le marché paysan
farmers market

le bruit
noise

soudain
sudden

le panier
basket

le trottoir
sidewalk

le berger
shepherd

**le chien
(la chienne)**
dog

la clope
slang for cigarette

le salon de coiffure
hairdresser's

le champ de vision
field of vision

la fleuriste
flower shop

la boulangerie
bakery

**ma chienne s'est
échappée!**
my dog got loose

la digue
seawall,
embankment

la brebis
sheep

le pot de colle
pot of glue,
a clingy dog

**Vous avez vu ma
chienne?
Ma chienne!**
Have you seen
my dog?

la trottinette
kick scooter

**le Ciotaden,
la Ciotadenne**
resident of
La Ciotat

pile-poil
right there

merci beaucoup
thanks a lot

3

BIEN JOUÉ

I really want to learn a new thing, but I do not know what I am interested in. UI/UX design? Being a certified therapist? Fashion? So much that I can or could be. Should I pretend to be someone until I am this person?

The above is an excerpt from a letter our daughter wrote one year ago. I am happy to announce we are all rejoicing now that she has passed her *examen oral* in Lyon—*la dernière étape* in a race to earn her BAC + 3, or bachelor's degree in one year. *Bien joué, Jackie!* You did it! You hunkered down, put your doubts and fears behind you, and traded your bartender apron for a student's cap. Then you proceeded to wow us all! *Tu nous as bluffés.*

I admit when you shared you were going to study UX/UI design, I was doubtful: did you say computer coding was part of the curriculum? I had similar misgivings when you dropped out of fashion in Toulon to go to bartending school in Miami. But if there's one thing about you, it's this: once you know what you want, your determination follows. I watched you line up everything, lightning speed: you located *un logement* in Lyon, turned in

all your papers at *le pôle emploi* (to the stellar counselor who found you this intensive program and knew you could do it), packed your belongings, sold some things and once again headed off into the unknown in search of who you might become.

Then, the first setback. After quitting your job, you got a call informing you that you were rejected from the program! Was this a sign? Some of us here at home whispered we didn't think computer design was right for you, but you remained calm. You called the director to ask *why?* You told him you were very interested in this program and to please reconsider your candidature. Meantime you looked for a last-minute employment and tried to stay out from underneath that cloud that forms above you during transition time, dark as the inside of a cocoon before the butterfly struggles out and takes flight.

Friends talked you into a weekend getaway. You had just landed in London when your phone rang at the airport. You almost ignored the call, but finally answered. It was the school director. Having had a second look at your *dossier*, he decided to give you a chance. Class started in less than a week!

You hung up the phone and quickly called back the rental company. The room was still available! You flew home and boarded the train to Lyon.

You were the first to arrive at the renovated house-turned-apartments in Villeurbanne, never suspecting the strangers now filing into the common space (it was their first night in these new digs, too) would become friends for life: a young doctor from Saudi Arabia, a computer programmer, a student musician, two nurses, a nuclear engineer, a biochemist, a dental hygienist, a logistics specialist, a shop manager/wedding photographer, and an agronomist (ahem, a weed producer).

You had me laughing when your biggest concern the first day of school was switching out your rickety chair for the one across the classroom you'd already set your sights on. I now see it as a metaphor....

At 25, you always considered yourself *une mauvaise élève*: a dreamer with severe test anxiety. But you set your mind on overcoming these obstacles and soon you had that chair, and more. You wasted no time choosing your project (your mock business was a cruise company for seniors), and you threw your heart, soul, and sweat into designing your logo, your app, your webpage, and interviewing seniors (your grandparents included).

The calendar ahead was challenging, three years of work crammed into one—including an internship (it was up to you to find the company, *dare-dare!*). Six months into the program and the pressure was unbearable: you wondered how you were going to turn in your preliminary report, finish your internship at the PR company, print out all your work in a series of booklets, and create your PowerPoint presentation. *C'était la mer à boire!* A bitter and impossible feat!

When at the 11th hour you had a panic attack at the PR office and an ambulance took you to the ER you might have had a good reason to call it quits.... After all, was this accelerated program worth the toll it was taking on your nervous system?

Back home we held our collective breath. "Jackie is tough! She's a Marcus!" Grandma Jules reminded us. Meantime, there in Lyon, your roommates rallied around you, gathering in your shared liv-

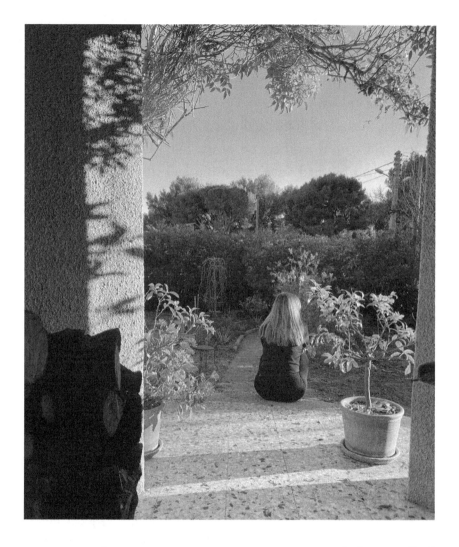

ing room to hear you practice your 50-minute speech for your final exams before *un jury*. They took notes and shared "improvements".

You made it home for a needed rest at Christmas. After four days you wasted no time returning to Lyon. You had to find *une imprimerie* to print out your final project, including four bound reports of the 200 pages you had carefully written, and present it before the real jury. You buckled down to business and we did not hear from you again. *Le silence radio…*

On January 10th you called me unexpectedly. I braced myself as it was your exam day. "Hi Mom, I'm on my way to the hairdresser's."

"The hairdresser's? But shouldn't you be cramming for your exam?"

Your voice on the other end of the line was so peaceful. Now that you had finished your internship and turned in your work, the intense pressure had subsided. As for your presentation for your oral exam, you knew your subject like the back of your hand. Speaking of which…

"I also got my nails done," you said. "*Je vais mettre toute les chances de mon côté.* I'm putting all chance on my side and presentation is important!"

Well, I couldn't argue with that, and I hung up the phone with a big smile on my face. I knew right then you would be OK.

Still, I held my breath until you called back that afternoon to say "*Ça y est. Ça s'est bien passé!*"

"Well, what did they say?"

"They said I'm ready to do a Master's!"

Voilà, dear reader. I hope you enjoyed this happy update. Jackie is still waiting for the official news, the confirmation that she will receive her *certificat* (it is the equivalent of a BAC +3 *diplôme*) from the vocational school in Lyon. Meantime she finished the challenging UX/UI design program, having met all of the requirements. *Bien joué, ma fille*! You got that chair and now you'll get the graduation cap!

FRENCH VOCABULARY

bien joué!
good job!

un examen oral
oral exam

la dernière étape
the last step

BAC + 3
Bachelor degree

Tu nous as bluffés
you blew us away

un logement
accommodation,
housing

le pôle emploi
the employment
center

le dossier
portfolio

**un(e) mauvais(e)
élève**
a bad student

dare-dare
right away

**C'est la mer à
boire**
it's like drinking
the entire sea,
no small feat

un jury
examinations board

une imprimerie
printer's

le silence radio
radio silence

**mettre toutes
les chances
de son côté**
to put all chance
on one's side

ça y est
that's it

ça s'est bien passé
everything
went well

voilà
there you have it

le certificat
certificate

le diplôme
diploma

**Bien joué,
ma fille!**
Well done, my girl!

FEBRUARY
Février

FEBRUARY

4

CONGÉ

Salut! Ça va? My two-week *congé* is over and I am home now in France—back to the murmur of French, to the scent of the Mediterranean Sea, to bright yellow mimosa and extended family. Sunday's *cousinade*, or gathering with the cousins near Aix-en-Provence, was a joyous occasion even if I am still queasy with *le décalage horaire*. Surely jet lag was responsible for the confusion when my aunt-in-law, Annie, said I could set down the dirty dishes *dans le potager*. Now for me, potager means "*vegetable garden*," but who am I to question the authority of *une véritable* countrywoman?

Balancing a stack of dessert plates, I was headed to the garden when doubt stopped me in my tracks. This time I consulted Cousin Sabine."*Dis*, Annie tells me the dirty dishes go in the *potager*?"

"Ah," Sabine laughed, "*Maman* is referring to *le comptoir*! We call that *le potager*." *Voilà*, dear reader, an old-fashioned term for you the next time you're referring to the kitchen counter!

I spent a lot of time at the kitchen counter—er, *le potager*—back in the States, where my daughter Jackie and I had the chance to spend time with our American family. This short and sweet *réunion de famille* began with a brief stop in Denver, where my sister Heidi nurtured us back from *desynchronosis* or "time zone syndrome". While filling up on everything from homemade tacos to spaghetti and meatballs, I savored time with my nephew and niece, Payne and Reagan, who came home from the University of Colorado Boulder for a visit, before Jackie and I Ubered back to the airport, headed for California. I was on my way to the desert on a very specific mission: to hug my dad.

While family back home often reassure me the phone is marvelous technology, *rien ne vaut une bonne câlinade*—nothing compares to holding your loved ones close. So, after several *câlins* back in Colorado, it was time to hug a few more family members.

My little sister, Kelley, flew in from Washington State, followed by Heidi, and we spent four memorable days in Palm Springs with Dad and *belle-mère* Marsha, enjoying lots of time at *le potager*, chatting at the kitchen counter, and lots and lots of hugs! But the best was seeing Dad looking so fit, healthy, and happy, *grâce à son épouse*, Marsha, who is also a doting hostess to us girls. And it was great to finally enjoy our "coffee with Kristi" as Dad calls our father-daughter chats, in the same room instead of on different continents, technology permitting.

Over breakfast of fruit and Raisin Bran, I watched Dad toss blueberries directly from the carton into his bowl. "Dad, don't you wash the pesticides off those berries?" My father smiled: "I think the body does a good job sorting these things out. I'm not worried." I admire Dad's relaxed attitude and realize all the stress of keeping my food clean is more harmful than a handful of unwashed berries. It's these bits of no-nonsense wisdom, and Dad's endearing presence, I miss so much…and the fact I can't see the blueberries, i.e., those little things he does daily that speak of his *philosophie de vie*. So, I soak in as much together-time as possible and make a vow with my sisters to visit more often.

While chasing each other in golf carts, accompanying Dad and Jasper to the dog park, or gathering around the *potager/comptoir*… we all seized the chance to laugh, shed a few tears, and encourage each other. All of these are important for an *expatriée*, for anyone living an ocean apart from loved ones. Yes, the telephone is a marvelous invention (and WhatsApp and FaceTime, too) but those warm hugs are vital. *Rien ne vaut un bon câlin.*

FRENCH VOCABULARY

le congé
vacation

salut
hi

ça va
how are you?

la cousinade
reunion of cousins

le décalage horaire
time difference,
jet lag

le potager
kitchen garden,
kitchen counter
(in old Provençal)

une véritable
a true

Dis
say

Maman
Mom

le comptoir
the counter

voilà
there you have it

**la réunion de
famille**
family reunion

la câlinade
a made-up word
for hug fest

le câlin
hug

la belle-mère
stepmother,
mother-in-law

la Californie
California

grâce à son épouse
thanks to his wife

**la philosophie
de vie**
life philosophy

un(e) expatrié(e)
an expatriate

FEBRUARY

5

PANCARTE

The last moments before Jean-Marc flew to New Zealand for his wine mission were spent fixing our plumbing. Ever since we moved to this 1960s villa in August 2017, we've been walking a fine, crooked line with our abominable *système d'évacuation WC*. It all boils down to the snaking path of our *canalisations*, the stubborn corners of which create blockage from the build-up of *papier toilette*. Repairing the problem could involve ripping out our floors to locate the crooked pipes and reroute them. The demolition involved could be extensive and I don't want to destroy our floors. So, we have remained as stuck as our *bouchon* as we tiptoe around the problem, being *soucieux* with what we put in the toilet. Easy for us, but try getting family and guests to behave.

(While we are here, dear reader, and just to add to your French vocabulary, here are seven things not to toss in the toilet: *lingettes humides, cotons-tiges, serviettes hygiéniques, cheveux, préservatifs, mouchoirs en papier, et couches jetables*.)

"I think one of the kids' friends tossed a tampon in here," Jean-Marc suspects, after our pipes become clogged again (as evidenced by water rising unnervingly close to the toilet rim).

"Well, we don't know that," I say, defending *la coupable*. I like to believe people think before tossing just anything into a toilet, but my husband is right: the truth is many don't! We have discovered everything from plastic Q-tips to chicken bones in our toilet bowl! (Regarding the bones, for years I pinned the blame on a senior family member but, come to think of it, it happened when several workers were renovating our house, stopping at noon for lunch… *poulet rôti?*).

While we know better than to flush feminine products, I was astonished when our plumber advised us not to put *le PQ* into the *cuvette*. Well then, what did he expect us to do? "*Prenez une douche,*" he suggested. "You might take a shower after. It's what I do…."

I tried very hard not to picture our plumber following his own advice. Meantime, as our toilet is located in a separate room from our *salle de bains*, did he really think we were going to hop on over to the shower to rinse off? Honestly! Sometimes I think France is still living in *le Moyen Âge*.

What with this non-flushing fiasco, Jean-Marc and I have become part-time plumbers in the seven years we've been here, with one of us manning the garden hose and the other on standby beside the toilet. Removing a heavy metal grate from the back porch, my husband feeds *le tuyau* as far into our pipes as possible then releases a jet of water whilst inside the house I listen for the familiar glug, glug, glug of I'm not sure what. Then comes the call, "*VAS-Y! TIRE!*" With that, I flush the upstairs toilet, then hurry down the stairs to pull the chain on the other *WC*. (Ideally, one person is stationed at each toilet, but often there are only two of us here. Even so, I don't like to ask guests for help with this chore…)

When my sister and the kids visited last summer, Jean-Marc reminded me to tell my family NOT to put TP in the toilet. "But they'll think we are barbaric!" I argued. (For being so anti-barbaric I was rewarded with a grizzly midnight shift during the family visit as Jean-Marc and I snuck out to the backyard and pumped the pipes when all the toilets became stopped up!)

As the years passed, and our pesky plumbing problem persisted, I began dreaming of one of those Totos or Japanese toilets with the built-in water jets. But at 3000 euros a unit (and not all plumbers know how to install them) I researched other options. As stressful as this situation is, it's brought forth a few discoveries. For one, I've found the *HappyPo*—a portable douche that allows you to skip toilet paper altogether. And let me tell you, even if we move on to another house and the perfect plumbing system, I will forever have my *HappyPo* with me in the *WC*. And you should too! This *douche de fesses* is especially helpful for those suffering from *petits soucis* (such as hemorrhoids).

At D-12 hours until his departure for New Zealand, we hang up the towel and agree, whether we believe it or not, that the plumbing is somewhat fixed again. So, while Jean-Marc finished packing his bags, I had a nap. No sooner did my head hit the pillow than I heard my husband ripping piece after piece of tape…a familiar sound! Noooo…. He can't possibly be using duct tape (his solution to everything from broken bumpers to ripped hammocks) to fix our plumbing problem? My mind was alive with images and scenarios of our duct-taped toilet until, exhausted, I fell asleep.

When I woke up, I'd forgotten all about the tape until I entered the bathroom. And there, taped to the wall and also to the door, a handwritten *pancarte*. (So that's what he was doing…) The first word was giant and in red: "ZERO" and the next words were in his characteristic cursive: ZERO *papiers, serviettes…dans le WC. Merci d'utiliser la poupelle. Sorry. Merci.*" ZERO toilet paper, pads…in the toilet. Sorry. Thanks.

I found the all-caps, red-lettered note jarring (not to mention it riled my aesthetic sensibilities to see a sign like that at home). Finally, deep down, I didn't want this to be the last message I see before my man leaves (to think we once exchanged love notes!). But my emotions were overcome by amusement on noticing a slight error in the text. In the haste to tie up so many loose ends before his departure, my husband had scribbled a "p" instead of a "b"…so that *poubelle* (garbage can) read "*poupelle*".

(*Pardonnez-moi* for all this toilet talk, dear reader, but I can't stop laughing over the accidental exactitude of *poupelle*—for isn't that where the plumber was suggesting we put the toilet paper? And didn't it all add up to that?)

Back to the handwritten *pancarte*. Ah well, it wasn't the love letter of times past. And though I planned to rip it down as soon as my husband left, I've decided to keep it posted on the bathroom wall, that all-caps plea in Valentine-red ink. After all, it is a lively, caring, and protective sentiment all the same, one I can hold on to. Now if only our *WC* could learn to let go….

FRENCH VOCABULARY

la pancarte
sign

le système d'évacuation WC
the toilet drainage system

le WC
toilet

la canalisation
pipe

le papier toilette
toilet paper

le bouchon
blockage

soucieux, soucieuse
careful, mindful

les lingettes humides
baby wipes

le coton-tige
Q-tip

la serviette hygiénique
sanitary pad

le cheveu
hair

le préservatif
condom

le mouchoir en papier
tissue

la couche jetable
disposable diaper

le/la coupable
the guilty party

le poulet rôti
roast chicken

le PQ (le papier Q)
toilet paper

la cuvette
toilet bowl

prenez une douche
take a shower

la salle de bains
bathroom

le Moyen Âge
the Middle Ages

le tuyau
pipe

vas-y!
go ahead!

tire!
flush!

la douche de fesses
shower for the bottom

les petits soucis
little worries

merci d'utiliser la poupelle
thanks for using the garbage

la poubelle
the garbage can

*A*s I type this *billet*, my daughter is flying over the Atlantic, halfway between New York and Paris. Jackie's been away four weeks, on the road and in the air since earning her B+3 Bachelor's degree in Lyon. (Ça y est! It's official: we have a graduate!)

Such freedom after buckling down for the intensive program must feel *revigorante*. After receiving her UI (user interface) degree, our 26-year-old flew from Marseille to Denver, on to Palm Springs, then to Tulum (*le Mexique*) where she zipped around on a scooter (mama mia!), then onto her old stomping grounds in Miami, and finally to New York City where former Florida roommate, Ruby, offered *un canapé* to sleep on and a snuggly Shiba Inu. (How Jackie longed to sneak the puppy into her *bagage en cabine* before leaving.)

Soon my youngest will land in Paris for a several-hour layover. At *Aéroport Charles de Gaulle* she'll have plenty of time to think about her next move (more schooling? A job? Or more travel before settling down?). Meantime I'm wondering just what she will do in the Paris airport with all that time on her hands? What healthy alternatives are there to do in any international airport besides drop more money and eat at Chuck E. Cheese (Is there a Chuck E. Cheese in Paris? I know my daughter was asking about it when nostalgia had her revisiting her favorite childhood haunts on her US visit).

But back to costly airport layovers—a subject I've been obsessed with lately (more about that in a bit). A visit online at ParisAéroport.fr reveals a thousand ways to spend-while-you-wait for your connecting flight. From food to fancy *fringues*, if you're not careful with your *porte-monnaie* your vacation could end up costing even more than you bargained for.

Beginning with food…Brioche Dorée, Ladurée (pastries and candy…), McDonald's, Starbucks—unless you've managed to hijack a sandwich from the previous flight (and pockets full of pretzels from the cocktail cart), these airport eateries will be your pricey alternatives.

One could always stick to water. But have you seen the price of airport H2O? I don't know about Paris, but a tiny bottle of water was $6 when I landed in Frankfurt two weeks ago. It sent me on a nostalgic hunt for the nearest water fountain (located just across the mall from one of the Frankfurter hotdog stands).

After you've eaten, you might be tempted by all the airport boutiques—a most dangerous way to pass the time! One more warning: jet lag is like being drunk—your senses are not as sharp. This is not a good time to be making costly decisions. Meantime Bulgari, Céline, Gucci, Dior, and more line the Paris airport walkways like pricey little traps. A young woman with a credit card could get in trouble!

Say you manage to skip the overpriced food and tempting boutiques (including the glittering *joailleries*)—just what is there to do for all those terminally long hours in an airport terminal, international or otherwise? Some sort of healthy activity would be ideal. But what—beyond walking in circles—is available beneath the friendly skies that won't take your wallet for a ride?

They say business is about finding a need and filling it. And this, dear reader, got me thinking about a side gig. Lately, it's been a struggle to keep this blog up and "flying", and now with a sharp decline in readership, I wonder what tomorrow holds. Fifteen years ago, at its peak, this French Word-A-Day newsletter had 50,000 subscribers from all over the world. And now I watch with growing alarm as dozens unsubscribe each week. This journal is becoming a shadow of its former self—even the old saying *If you build it, they will come* no longer seems to apply when readers are rushing elsewhere. But where?

Part of me (the part that doesn't take things too personally) suspects that with the growth of social media, readers are migrating north, leaving the warm shores of the blogosphere for a thrilly-chilly dose of whatever the Algorithm Gods serve up on Instagram—anything to keep us addicted to bite-size bits of information. When I lament about the future of blogging, my tech-savvy daughter tells me, "You've got to keep up with the times, Mom!" But how to keep up with the times *as a writer*? Isn't writing timeless?

And so I've begun dreaming up a side-gig—*un petit boulot supplémentaire*—something outside the writing sphere but with the familiar rhythm and beat that keeps my soul singing and my mind dancing. There you have it, dear reader—sphere, rhythm, beat, dancing—a few hints, clues, or indices regarding an idea that's taken a seat in my mind. You might say a seat amidst thousands in a bustling airport terminal. In the next five weeks, I'll flesh out this novel idea and report back to you at the beginning of April. For now, *cha-cha-cha!* Time to get up and make a move!

FRENCH VOCABULARY

un indice
clue, hint

le billet
post, blog post

ça y est
that's it

revigorant,e
invigorating

le canapé
couch, sofa

le Mexique
Mexico

le bagage en cabine
carry-on bag

**l'Aéroport
Charles de Gaulle**
Charles de Gaulle
Airport

les fringues
threads (clothing)

le porte-monnaie
wallet

la joaillerie
jewelry store

**un petit boulot
supplémentaire**
a side gig

FEBRUARY

7

CANULAR

*G*etting cozy on the couch with a cup of tea and our Shepherd, Ricci, I watched my daughter prepare to leave for her brother's pour *rendre un service*.

Grabbing the car keys Jackie turned to me, "Mom, why don't you come along to Max's? We can walk Ana's dog while she's away." Visions of climbing four flights of stairs to my son's condo (to lead a scent-obsessed Beagle on a kilometer-long promenade) had me sinking back into the sofa. "*J'ai la flemme*," I admitted.

"Energy comes in moving!" Jackie countered.

Don't you love it when young people share their wisdom? Jackie is right. I needed to shake up my afternoon routine. Some salty fresh air and, though I didn't know it yet, a little mischievous behavior, would be *vivifiant* for body, mind, and soul, and who could have guessed the positive effect would ripple out and tickle somebody else in the process....

If my daughter managed to rouse me, the drive to her brother's fired up every nerve ending in my being as I gripped the handle above the passenger door. "Jackie, slow down! Don't follow so close to the other cars! DID YOU SEE THE PEDESTRIAN???"

Speaking of pedestrian, between beginning today's story and procrastinating its development, I came across the word "pedestrian" and was amused by its various meanings:

1. lacking wit or imagination
2. walking

Isn't it interesting how the very act of walking stirs creative intelligence? Perhaps this explains how, after marching from the car to Max's condominium and up four flights of stairs, a creative urge came over me. The urge to play a practical joke on my son. Normally void of ideas for these kinds of *bêtises*, my mind was now reeling with possibilities.

A look around Max's home revealed he's been struggling to keep up with *le ménage* ever since he began his new job two months ago. On top of domestic challenges, he's been exhausted from keeping on top of a new job. A little prank might perk him up.

"Jackie!" I giggled. "Do you know what a practical joke is?"

"No…"

"I'll show you…Let's turn everything in Max's fridge upside down! Here…" I said, opening the door, "Start with the condiments…" While Jackie upended the ketchup, mayo, and pickles, I grabbed a bowl. "Let's put the jar of *cornichons* in here in case it leaks. We just want to have fun—not flood his apartment," I said, bummed that we couldn't turn over the bottles of beer because of their narrow tops.

As Jackie turned her attention to the shelves, putting everything the wrong way up, I carefully flipped the bowl of onions, peppers, and herbs on the counter, and then made my way over to the spices. *Les épices* were lined up neatly at the back of *la table de cuisson*, but not for long…

After we'd somersaulted everything in the *frigo* and around the stove, I headed to Max's room when Jackie suggested we stop. *Elle avait raison.* We'd made our mischievous mark; besides, there'd be more occasions in which to mess with Max. Especially after he retaliated—no doubt he would!

With a pat on the back we left Izzy the Beagle, swearing her to secrecy: *Chut! Ne dis rien!* "Now Izzy, don't tell Max what you saw!" With that, we returned home for dinner…. and waited for a call from Max, eager to know his reaction.

Finally, the phone rang, but our victim didn't mention anything amiss.

"Where are you?" Jackie quizzed.

"I'm in the basement, organizing some things."

"Oh, anything else new?"

"No," Max replied with a yawn. Jackie and I were feeling let down until an afterthought from Max stirred us again: "By the way, did you turn over that bowl on my countertop?"

"No…" Jackie responded. Giving me a thumbs up as she spoke into the receiver. "I don't know what you are talking about."

"*Bon*," Max said, sounding bored. "I've gotta finish up here. Talk to you later." We were sure we'd get a call back, but the night wore on, and not a word from Max.

Meantime, I began to doubt our *farce*. Was it not clever? But then, a brilliant practical joke isn't about cleverness—its appeal lies in timing. Was this bad timing?

The next day I nearly bypassed the morning prayer to open text messages first thing. The little devil in me was desperate to know if Max had discovered the full extent of our friendly trespass. Surely by now he would have seen the contents of his fridge *mis à l'envers*.

Still no word from him, I tried to be coy with my message. "Hey, Son. Do you know the term "topsy turvy?"

(No response.)

"Things feeling a little upside-down over there?" I persisted.

Finally, my phone chimed! "I saw your joke," the text read. My son's deadpan response killed it—that wonderful creative buzz born of a pedestrian effort.

"But Max," I despaired, "didn't you think it was funny?"

"Sure."

Sure?

"He's just tired," Jackie remarked when I couldn't let go—until finally I did. I let go of the fish. In French *un poisson* is synonymous with "practical joke" or *farce*. But it may as well be synonymous with "the outcome of things". It reminds me of the would-be thrill and adventure of writing: the reward, it turns out, lies not in the outcome but in the golden nuggets we gather along the way. This story (and the fun and games behind it) was born of one child's wisdom and the other's wisecrackery. Indeed, the old Max will be back. Once he gets the hang of his new job, he'll be back at our home, setting all kinds of traps for the family. After all, we learned these pranks from him—even more, Max has shown us time and again how *les badinages* and *plaisanteries* are a good way not to take ourselves too seriously.

Meantime, let the outcome be the uncontrollable outcome. Continue to work, love, learn, and especially to have fun.

FRENCH VOCABULARY

un canular
practical joke

rendre un service
to help out

j'ai la flemme
I'm feeling lazy

vivifiant
invigorating

une bêtise
mischief

le ménage
housework

les cornichons
pickles

les épices
spices

la table de cuisson
stovetop

le frigo
fridge

elle avait raison
she was right

Chut! Ne dis rien!
Hush, don't say
a word!

bon
alright

une farce
practical joke

mis à l'envers
put upside down

un poisson
fish

le badinage
banter

la plaisanterie
joke

MARCH
Mars

8
AVOIR
DU CRAN

*D*o you believe that our behavior can provoke the universe? I can't help but wonder when, hours before her eye exam, Mom appears in my room and declares, "I do not want any more doctors' appointments!"…only to be issued, hours later, a slew of new *rendez-vous*.

Whether or not our conduct stirs the Powers That Be, it moves mere mortals. Not sure how to respond to my mom (or how to deal with the let-down), I choose to reason with her: "But Mom, how many doctor visits have you had in the last year?" I challenge, knowing well we've not suffered more than a handful—one or two times to the family *toubib*, to renew a prescription, and two *aller-retours* to the *ophtalmo* after severe pain revealed too much pressure in Mom's eye. But never mind the facts, Jules's mind was made up.

"I'm not going!"

"Mom! We can't cancel. We're going!"

Sensing some sort of diatribe on my part, Jules quietly exits, shutting the door behind her, against which I unleash a string of *gros mots*: @#%!! @#%!! @#%!!

Well, that got her attention. Mom returns. We exchange stubborn looks. I offer an *"I'm sorry but…!"*

I'm sorry but *do you realise I've arranged my day around this eye exam?* I'm sorry but *do you know how hard it is to get a doctor's appointment anymore?* I'm sorry but *I am the one handling your healthcare as you don't speak French or drive!*

Suddenly, Mom approaches the bed to sit beside me. After a few deep breaths, we are on a walk down memory lane as visions of our life back at the trailer park come flooding forth—including the time Jules tossed our toys out the window after my sister's and my roughhousing damaged our family's new bean bag, spilling *les haricots* all over the living room. Mom had her *gros mot* moments @#%!! but who could blame her as she struggled to raise two girls on her own while working full-time? And yet somehow this single mother managed. Even more, Mom signed us up for Brownies, Girl Scouts, gymnastics, and band, and somehow managed to buy everything from my clarinet to my sister's first car. When my sister had a car accident Mom nursed her back to life and made Heidi return to school to finish the year, despite the scars from several broken bones, in time to go on to college. Heidi became the first one in Jules's family to graduate from college, and with a degree in journalism! Meantime Jules's worries weren't over: her youngest (*moi-même*) dropped out of community college and returned home. (I eventually followed in my sister's footsteps, graduating from college with a degree in French, and began writing after moving to France.)

"All I want now is peace and quiet," Mom admits, as we sit in bed holding hands, hours before her doctor's appointment. "I am so grateful to live here with you and not to have to worry any longer."

Turning to Mom, I would like to say I understand the struggle and that, at 56, I'm tired too! But one must press on! Only, unlike Mom, I have not been worn down from the stress of trying to pay for ice skates, braces, or clothes at the beginning of each school year. Through it all, we never received the admonition, "Money doesn't grow on trees!" Instead, Jules instilled a work ethic that had my sister and me earning first an allowance, then cash from babysitting and a paper route, and finally our first paycheck jobs by the age of fifteen.

"And now here we are in France!" Mom whispers, squeezing my hand. It never ceases to amaze Mom that she is living on the Riviera after surviving in the desert. (Our neighborhood was a senior citizen mobile home park, but Mom convinced the landlord to let us in as she was the first to rent a space when it opened. We stayed 11 years. Before it was demolished, we moved on, and Mom eventually settled into a beautiful cabin near Saguaro Lake. Then to Mexico for 22 years before coming to live with us in France.)

"I am so proud of my daughters," Mom says, turning to me. Jules has kindly forgotten my earlier slur of cuss words and a peaceful truce is once again underway. This wasn't the first and won't be our last mother-daughter fender-bender, but we have acquired some tools to hammer out the dents along the way—our shared vulnerability being one of them. Another is forgiveness. Finally, there's grit—the French call it "*le cran*". Indeed, it takes courage and endurance to love and to keep on loving. I love you, Mom. *This one's for you.*

Update: we made it to the doctor's appointment in time for Mom's follow-up eye exam. The good news is her eye pressure has stabilized. But she now has to undergo a series of shots to treat the edema, or swelling, inside her right *oeil*. For that, Jackie will drive her grandma to Marseille. Wish Mom luck as the first eye injection is today!

My beautiful Mom, in the doctor's waiting room, gazing out the window to the Mediterranean. I will always be moved by Mom's strength, courage, and perseverance in the face of so many challenges. *Elle a du cran!* The French would say. She has guts!

FRENCH VOCABULARY

avoir du cran
to be brave

le rendez-vous
appointment

le toubib
doctor

aller-retour
round trip

**l'ophtalmo
(l'ophtalmologue)**
eye doctor

la diatribe
tirade, rant

le gros mot
swear word

les haricots
beans

moi-même
myself

Elle a du cran
She has guts!

l'oeil
eye

9
FRIANDISE

*I*n the *salle d'attente* at the eye clinic in Marseille, everyone is wearing shower caps. A male nurse breezes in, administers eye drops to a half-dozen patients, and disappears. A faint scent of iodine lurks in the air—evidence everyone has (hopefully) followed instructions to shower with *Betadine* the night before and day of the ocular intervention. So much scrubbing seems a bit drastic given patients remain fully clothed during the 10-minute procedure to treat a certain *pathologie oculaire* caused by macular degeneration. I wonder, did Mom remove her hat? I had a lot of questions, but having delegated Jules's doctor's visit to my daughter, I would not know every detail of the intervention. But I did get as much info as possible, so on with our story…

Back at *Clinique Chantecler*, Jackie, also wearing a shower cap, is sitting beside her *grand-mère*. For the entire ride to Marseille, Jules sat quietly in the passenger seat, nervously filing her nails (hard as a rock from the potassium tablets the *opthalmo* prescribed for her eye tension). The male nurse reappears, asking all the patients to hand over the box with the aflibercept injection they were prescribed (to be stored at home in the refrigerator and brought to today's appointment). Not surprisingly, half the room has forgotten to bring the medicine. Did they leave the box beside the cheese and the *cornichons*…as we might have? No, too many precautions were taken here at home…in the form of numerous sticky notes strategically placed around our house, in addition to my phone alarm. While I did entrust my daughter with expediting Grandma to the clinic, I didn't leave every detail to her.

Jackie dug through her bag, where, beside her grandmother's medical folder, and her immigrant insurance card, she located the shot box.

"*Merci, Mademoiselle,*" the nurse smiled. Little did Jackie know she was earning brownie points for later, when her calm demeanor would earn her special hospital privileges. Turning her attention back to Grandma, who is feeling anxious about the upcoming needle in the eye, Jackie is reassuring: "Don't worry. I'm sure it will go quickly, Grandma. After, I'll take you for ice cream!"

The other patients, mostly senior citizens, seem intrigued by the two foreigners. One of them reaches out: "*Votre grand-mère est anglaise?*" Your grandmother is English?

"*Non. Elle est américaine,*" Jackie answers. "*Elle a un peu peur.*" With that, the other patients are quick to offer comforting words:

"*Oh, c'est rien!*" says the woman with the plastic shield over her eye. Another adjusts his surgical cap, "*Vous verrez, ça ne fait pas mal du tout.*" The woman with a bandage agrees: "*Je viens ici chaque mois.*" The youngest in the group, a businessman here during his lunch hour, smiles warmly, "*C'est comme une lettre à la poste!*"

Jackie translates each encouragement. "You see, Grandma. It'll be as easy as posting a letter!" But there was no time to explain the postal expression as Jules was soon summoned to the eye injection chamber. (If words could paint Mom's imagination at this point…)

"*Mademoiselle, vous pouvez accompagner votre grand-mère.*" Good news, the doctor just made an exception to the patients-only rule, by allowing Jackie to assist her grandmother during the treatment.

(The next ten minutes were not so bad, Mom would later tell me. The hardest part was you had to watch the needle as it approached your eye…)

After the procedure, the foreigner and her *petite-fille* waved goodbye to the patients in the *salle d'attente*. At this point, Jackie might've patted herself on the back. But you know the saying: "No good deed goes unpunished"! After helping Grandma back into the passenger seat, our Do-Gooder got locked out of the electric car! Now the challenge was for Jules, with one eye bandaged, to find the door handle. But even after the struggle to locate the *poignée de porte*, the punishment wasn't over. Our little Renault Zoe would not start. A few deep breaths later (and surely some bionic praying on Grandma's part) Jackie solved the problem by removing the electronic key from its case and using it instead of the dashboard button.

The third strike came when Jules began to suffer a sudden *mal de tête*. Jackie, our quick-thinking *ambulancière*, wound the seat back as far as it would go, and soon Grandma fell asleep, only to wake when the two reached *le péage* in La Ciotat. Before Jules could remember her pain, Jackie reminded her of *la friandise* she'd promised.

Soon after, I received an update from McDonald's drive-through, "Here in 10," my daughter's text read. "The ice cream's on you, lol, I don't have the money."

I laughed, remembering Jackie had my Paypal debit card from when she did the grocery shopping earlier. I was so relieved the eye intervention was over that I couldn't have cared if the duo ordered sundaes for everyone in line—and knowing Mom she would! Finally, my telephone chimed with a notification from Paypal that a charge of 7 euros just went through. Well, that was a good deal! After all, a medical cab would have cost many times the price, and it wouldn't have included a doting assistant or a visit to *MacDo**!

In retrospect, entrusting this special expedition to Jackie had been the right decision after all. Not only was it a needed lesson in delegation for me, but it was also an opportunity for grandmother and granddaughter to share meaningful time together. Jackie handled it all with professionalism, ensuring Grandma was in good hands throughout. And while I may not have indulged in a sundae myself, seeing the smiles on their faces was the sweetest reward of all.

FRENCH VOCABULARY

la friandise
a sweet treat

la salle d'attente
waiting room

Betadine
an antiseptic used
before and after
surgery

**la pathologie
oculaire**
eye pathology

la grand-mère
grandmother

**l'ophtalmo
(l'ophtalmologue)**
eye doctor

le cornichon
pickle

**Merci,
Mademoiselle**
Thanks,
Mademoiselle

**Votre grand-mère
est anglaise?**
Your grandmother
is English?

Elle est Americaine
She is American

Elle a un peu peur
She's a little afraid

C'est rien
It's nothing

vous verrez
you'll see

**ça ne fait pas
mal du tout**
it doesn't hurt at all

**Je viens ici
chaque mois**
I come here
each month

**C'est comme une
lettre à la poste**
It's (as simple) as
dropping off a letter
at the post office

**Vous pouvez
accompagner**
You can go with her

la petite fille
granddaughter

la poignée de porte
door handle

le mal de tête
headache

**l'ambulancier,
ambulancière**
ambulance driver

le péage
toll booth

MacDo
French slang for
McDonald's

10

FOU RIRE

*I*t's dusk and I'm alone at home, emptying the dishwasher. When Ricci suddenly starts barking, I look over at our *baie-vitrée* only to be startled by the sight of a figure looming beyond the glass, on the front patio. Our dog is yipping like crazy now, causing my heart to leap. *Qu'est-ce qui se passe? Qui est là?*

Ouf! Exhaling a sigh of relief, I recognize the young woman wearing sweatpants and a hoodie. Back now from her boxing class, it is only my "*coloc*," my roommate as she jokingly calls herself. I unlock the glass door to hear laughter on the other side. "Oh, Mom! You should've seen your face!"

"*Trop drôle!*" Har, har! I say, stepping aside to usher my daughter into the house. Noticing all the groceries, I wonder, hadn't I sent Jackie for some veggies and meat, *seulement*? Memories of my own antics when I lived with my dad flooded back—a time when I'd occasionally sneak in a *Vogue* magazine or some Maybelline mascara alongside our groceries, courtesy of Dad's credit card.

Still, I can't help but want to audit this latest grocery haul, and my daughter, as usual, can read my mind: "What's up, Mom?"

Jackie says, in her relaxed way. After two seconds of self-control, I blurt out my thoughts: "It's just that I hope you didn't buy things we already have…." That said, I resolve to keep the peace, even if I'm imploding inside. I regret I will always struggle to *lâcher prise*. But it's worth asking, now and then, just what is it I'm holding onto?

Meantime…

Given Carrefour supermarket has an extensive beauty section, I'm wondering if *un masque concombre purifiant* or another *soin intensif capillaire* got mixed in with our "groceries." I'll just have a peek, now and then, as Jackie puts away *les courses* and I resume unloading the dishwasher.

"Bread?" I say, looking over from the cupboard. "But we already have that."

"Mom, I want to make sandwiches this week," Jackie says, with a hint of exasperation. Is she tired of my one-pot meals? But they're convenient: make once and feast for days! Next, my volunteer shopper sets down a bunch of *citrons verts*…

"Jackie! What do you need 12 limes for?"

"I like to cook with them, and they're great in water," she explains, with a touch of mischief.

"Well, OK," I relent. "But you know I can't bear to toss out food."

"That I know!" Jackie laughs, recalling the 5-day-old chili I ate for breakfast. "I'll pray for you!" she had said. I was touched by my daughter's sudden piety…until I realized she was teasing me (she'd prayed I would survive the chili!).

(*Prout! Prout!* Evidence I'm still alive!)

Next, I stumble upon some cheese. "Parmesan. But we already have some!"

"I like the grated kind, Mom. It's for some carbonara I'm making you. *Allez, oust!* Go do something else!"

"OK. OK!" I'm a few steps out of the kitchen when… "By the way, how was your meeting at the fitness club in Marseille? Did you sign up?"

"It was great. Yes, I signed up," Jackie smiles.

"Did you pay three months upfront?"

"I did."

"You did!" I say, surprised by an involuntary, head-to-toe wiggle punctuating my words.

"Mom? What did that mean?" Jackie laughs, mimicking my wise-cracking wiggle.

"I don't know!" I play dumb, but my body language has already given me away. I can now see how uptight I am being—so much so my body's trying to wiggle me out of it!

"Just what was that?" Jackie teases, doing *The Wiggle* as she speaks, easing a few giggles out of me.

"Nothing, it's just…" I begin to laugh… "You spent the same amount on your gym membership as I just spent on groceries… and I guess I was trying to make a point!"

Wiggle, wiggle! Jackie illustrates she gets my point.

But of course, she does! She can read me like a book. Not only does she have a high emotional IQ, but she's street smart too, having weathered her share of *mésaventure*. After getting scammed in Miami and returning to France, Jackie has gradually built back her savings, her self-esteem, and enough trust in others to move on. That she can laugh this way today and encourage others to do the same is a testament to her strength. I can see it as we stand there bantering in the corner "ring" of our living room:

Jackie, still in her boxing attire, still laughing, performs a left-right punch to the air, signaling to me to loosen up a bit. Her antics are disarming and by now I'm laughing so hard my stomach muscles hurt. *Ça y est*, I think I know what it is I'm holding onto, after all: a lot of *fous rires*. It is clear I need to let go and laugh more often. And don't we laugh the hardest with the ones who know us best? Their message is the same: you've got to laugh at yourself, let go and let others help you to do so.

Prout! Prout! From here on out I vow to keep trying!

FRENCH VOCABULARY

le fou rire
the giggles

la baie-vitrée
sliding glass door

Qu'est-ce qui se passe? Qui est là?
What is going on?
Who is there?

ouf!
phew!

le/la coloc
housemate

trop drôle
ha ha (sarcasm)

seulement
only

lâcher prise
let go

un masque concombre purifiant
purifying cucumber mask

le soin intensif capillaire
intensive scalp treatment

les courses
groceries

le citron vert
lime

prout! prout!
toot! toot!

allez, oust!
go! get out of here!

la mésaventure
misfortune

Ça y est!
There it is

APRIL
Avril

11
BOUGEOTTE

t's the beginning of April and, a little while back, I promised an update about a side gig I am working on—*un petit boulot* to supplement my writing given that blog readership continues to dwindle. Finally, I have a few bits of news: the first is that Jean-Marc will be joining me in this venture. To understand just why he's the man, here is a little review of his career path before I reveal to you our new project:

After graduating with a degree in accounting, Jean-Marc made a career U-Turn to pursue a growing passion for winemaking. We left Marseille in 1995, after the birth of our son, for St. Maximin, where Jean-Marc became sales director for Château Ferry Lacombe. Next, a headhunter wooed him over to the prestigious Château Sainte Rosaline in Les Arcs-sur-Argens (where, incidentally, this blog began). From there our future *vigneron* did a brief stint at GAI (an Italian bottling machine manufacturer) before buying his first vineyard in Sainte Cécile-Les-Vignes where he made his first award-winning wines, including Lunatique. Five years later he acquired his dream vineyard near Bandol. (If you read our memoir, *The Lost Gardens: A Story of Two Vineyards and a Marriage*, you know how this ended.) Pulling himself back up by his rubber bootstraps, Jean-Marc stepped out of that bucket of grapes and into his first boutique, creating a successful wine shop here in La Ciotat—only to develop *la bougeotte*, itchy feet or wanderlust, once again! When Jean-Marc suddenly sold Le Vin Sobre in 2023, he left many of us wondering *just what would Chief Grape think up next?*

A little over a year later and he can finally spill the grapes....
Introducing "Bougeotte": Disco, Wine & Spirits Bar.

Combining three of his loves: travel, spirits, and dance, our intrepid traveler's comeback is sure to make a splash at the Paris Charles de Gaulle Airport where it is set to take off this fall. Catering to wine lovers and those who are looking for something physical to do during a 2-, 4-, 8-, or more-hour layover, the disco bar will be known for its pre-departure dance-a-thons.

Needless to say, we are all doing a happy dance, given a very real risk of losing our Chief to New Zealand (where several headhunters have already tried wooing the French winemaker over to their wine cellars once his contract at Whitehaven Winery is finished at the end of the month).

Working together as a family, this new boogie business fits neatly with the skills of each family member: our son Max (also in the wine business), graduate of Montpellier Business School, is securing the airport rental space and the alcohol license. Our daughter Jackie (former bartender), recent graduate in web design, is in charge of the bespoke drinks menu and the website, and Grandma Jules, after a recent slumber, is ready to put her people skills to use at the hostess stand. I offered to handle the coat/baggage check, where I can sit at a desk with my laptop and write (think of all the colorful characters I'll have for inspiration…). Ricci, our American Shepherd, will be our in-house emotional support dog for weary travelers and Max's girlfriend Ana, a *kinésithérapeute*, or physiotherapist, will advise on dance moves to combat the effects of long-haul travel. Finally, my sister-in-law, Cécile, a movie set builder, with skills in masonry and ironwork, will design the wooden dance floor and the main attraction: a fantastic wrought iron cage suspended in the air by a giant chain. We call it our safe haven for that customer wishing to consume more than a few drinks. Once their alcohol level returns to "well-behaved passenger" level, a door on the cage will spring open and our tipsy-no-more travelers will make it to their gate on time!

My best friend Susan, CEO of Critics Choice Vacations, is flying in on Saturday to help set up a CCV antenna booth, where we will be able to rebook passengers who, reeling from so many dancing endorphins, have decided to extend their Paris layover in time to join us for our Dimanche Dance-a-thon (Kristi's favorite as it is gospel music only on Sundays. Oh Happy Day!).

That reminds me, I am also in charge of communications and my first job is to program ChatGTP to write a press release. (See below.) Oh, and for those of you who have already reserved a Provence Vineyard Visit with Jean-Marc this summer, be assured Chief Grape (soon-to-be "Chief Disco") will honor every appointment through September 23rd when Bougeotte Disco, Wine & Spirits Bar opens. Better bring your dancing shoes because he's so excited about his new Paris project he's liable to *danser* le Mia. I leave you with our press release:

FOR IMMEDIATE RELEASE

Introducing Bougeotte: Paris's Newest Airport Disco Set to Open at Charles de Gaulle Airport

Paris, France – April 1st, 2024 – Travelers passing through Charles de Gaulle Airport will soon have a groovy new destination to unwind and dance away their travel fatigue. Bougeotte, an innovative airport disco conceptualized by renowned entrepreneur/winemaker Jean-Marc Espinasse, is set to open its doors on September 23rd, 2024.

Derived from the French term for a person who loves to move around or travel, Bougeotte promises to be a haven for jet-setters seeking a unique and energizing experience at the airport. Strategically located just after customs, the disco will offer travelers a refreshing escape before embarking on their onward journey.

One of Bougeotte's standout features (apart from "La Cage") will be its signature drinks menu, by Jackie Espinasse, curated to combat the effects of jet lag. Patrons can indulge in anti-inflammatory concoctions such as the "Melatonin Margarita" and the "Pistachio Pina Colada," specially crafted to rejuvenate weary travelers and set the mood for an unforgettable night (or day) of dancing.

In addition to its eclectic beverage selection, Bougeotte will feature a large-screen TV displaying dance moves tailored to alleviate the discomfort of long-haul flights, including the notorious "*jambes lourdes*" (heavy legs). Guests can follow along and shake off the weariness of travel, embracing the rhythm and energy of the disco.

Jean-Marc Espinasse, the visionary behind Bougeotte, expressed his excitement about the project, stating, "Bougeotte is more than just a disco; it's a sanctuary for travelers to unwind, connect, and immerse themselves in the joy of movement. We're thrilled to bring this innovative concept to Charles de Gaulle Airport and provide travelers with a memorable experience that transcends the ordinary—while sparing them from the usual airport money grabs, i.e. all those duty-free shops."

Bougeotte invites international travelers with an upcoming layover in Paris to join in the celebration of movement, music, and Mourvèdre. Mark your calendars for September 23rd, 2024, and prepare to experience the magic of Bougeotte at Charles de Gaulle Airport.

For more information, visit my blog, where I keep an archive of April Fools stories just like this one. *Alors, je t'ai eu?*

FRENCH VOCABULARY

un petit boulot a side gig	**le vigneron** winemaker	**les jambes lourdes** heavy legs
la bougeotte itchy feet / wanderlust	**la boutique** shop	**Alors, je t'ai eu?** So, did I get you? (Did you fall for it?)

APRIL

12

BUTÉ

It all started with an unusual stream of yippy yelps, followed by moaning, crying, and whining. Next, came the overly amorous advances toward our couch pillows, *les coussins*, and the realization our *chienne* was acting very odd lately.

It must be the breed, I shrugged. American shepherds are highly vocal, intelligent, and need a lot of attention and care, in addition to loads of *activité physique*. Perhaps Ricci wasn't getting enough exercise, now that Jean-Marc was away in New Zealand? My morning beach strolls and evening circles around the block were not enough to work out all that pent-up energy in our 3-year-old *toutou*.

But when the local male dogs began making a *demi-tour* along the boardwalk, bee-lining down to Ricci at the beach (their owners shouting "*Reviens*!") we began to suspect our dog was in heat again.

Jackie figured it out first: *"Elle est en chaleur!"*

"But it's only been two months since her last cycle," I said, unbelieving.

"Better take her to the doctor," Jackie urged.

A trip to *le véto* produced more than a few surprises. The first was an encounter with a reader of this journal, who revealed herself with a soft-spoken *Bonjour, Kristi.* I couldn't believe my ears

when I heard my name spoken by a stranger! Stéphanie was on her way out with her cat when, on our way in, we held open the door in time to make the connection. During a few *aller-retours* (there were a total of three cats to transfer to her car) we learned we were near neighbors!

"A bientôt pour un café!" Waving goodbye to our new friend, Jackie and I continued to the front desk, where we were led into the examination room with Ricci—just in time for surprises two and three…

Not only was our dog in heat, she was in the middle of *une grossesse nerveuse*—a phantom pregnancy—as evidenced by *le lait maternel* she was producing, and also by the *échographie*. The ultrasound also revealed water in her uterus. The vet explained that not only was this not safe, but it could affect fertility which made me wonder if this is why our dog—a former *chienne reproductrice*— was retired from breeding and put up for sale?

We made an appointment for an *Ovario-hystérectomie* (for a week later, the time for the "Finilac" medication to suppress or end the lactation) and then waited nervously until Ricci came out of surgery.

The past week, post-op, has been a challenge given our dog is one stubborn patient, refusing to drink enough or to "do her business" (*faire ses besoins*) as usual. But then this isn't business as usual, after an invasive procedure, and who wouldn't be bull-headed when struggling with a large plastic cone? While we call it an "Elizabethan collar," the French have their own shameful synonyms for the plastic contraption designed to keep dogs and cats from licking their surgical wounds:

1) *la collerette de la honte* (cone of shame)
2) *l'abat-jour* (lampshade)

While those are amusing terms, our cone-headed convalescent is not smiling. *Elle boude.* She's also refusing to come when I call her, obliging me to pick her up and haul her up and down the stairs. And, once in bed with me, she runs circles around the mattress like a bull in a china shop, her roughhousing punctuated by an abrupt KICK! as she settles beside me, finally, only to groan.

"She's such a drama queen!" Jackie laughs, seeing through the act. Because the moment we remove the cone, Ricci's humming-bird energy instantly returns. But put the cone back on again and she reverts to a slug....

She is stubborn! In fact, I think she wins The Most Stubborn among all our feisty family members. Just to be sure, I check with Jackie... "Who is the most stubborn? Grandma Jules or Ricci?"

"Grandma."

"Really?" I'm surprised. "Ok, who's next after Grandma and Ricci?"

"You!"

"Me?" (And here I thought I was a pushover!) "Oh well, stubborn people rock!"

"True!" Jackie laughed. Well, that makes Grandma Jules a rock star...and little Ricci a Rockette. As for the other stubborn members in our family, I'd say Max, Jackie, and Jean-Marc tie for 4th place!

Off now to cater to our doggie drama queen. One more week of the cone, er—*la collerette de la honte*—and Ricci can hold her silky head high again. I think I will be as relieved as my dog when that annoying, clumsy piece of plastic is finally removed. *Bon débarras!*

FRENCH VOCABULARY

buté
stubborn

le coussin
pillow

la chienne
female dog

l'activité physique
physical activity

le toutou
dog (in slang)

le demi-tour
U-turn

Reviens!
Come back!

Elle est en chaleur
she's in heat

**le véto
(Veterinaire)**
veterinarian

bonjour
hello

aller-retour
round-trip

**à bientôt pour
un café**
see you soon for
a coffee

**une grossesse
nerveuse**
a phantom
pregnancy

le lait maternel
breast milk

l'échographie
ultrasound,
sonogram

**une chienne
reproductrice**
female breeding dog

**l'ovario-
hystérectomie (f)**
ovariohysterectomy
(spaying)

faire ses besoins
do your business

**la collerette
de la honte**
cone of shame

l'abat-jour (m)
lampshade

elle boude
she's pouting

bon débarras!
good riddance!

13
JAMAIS DEUX SANS TROIS

ast week may have been the most challenging since my husband left for New Zealand. On Sunday, owing to an old and faulty *serrure* on our front door, I found myself locked out of the house upon returning from church. I hurried around the corner to Mom's, put all the groceries I'd just bought into her *frigo*, and ran back to carefully work the key lest it break inside the lock. Forty-five minutes later, the sluggish lock relented. *Quel miracle!* Another answered prayer, along with the relief of stepping into a cool house! Despite the initial victory, the week was full of trials, each day punctuated by some disaster or another, whether that was Ricci busting a stitch (she nibbled the area) following her operation or the bathroom sink leaking again. And can you believe it all ended with *un pneu crevé*?

I was lying in bed at week's end, agonizing about the car when my daughter came into the room. It was 11 at night and she'd just finished a long shift at a bar in Cassis. "Don't worry about the flat tire, Mom. I'll take care of it." The next day Ms. Fix-It bought one of those aerosol tire inflators—*le dépanne-crevaison* for 15 bucks (everyone should have one in their *bagnole*!), filled the tire with air, and drove to a nearby garage to have both back tires changed. Next, she phoned Max's girlfriend, Ana, to ask her to drive Grandma and me to the next appointment in Gardanne. (Having unknowingly pierced the tire on the way home from Thursday's rendez-vous, Jules and I were lucky the tire didn't burst, sending us skidding across the *autoroute*!)

"Mom, you are out of practice. Let Ana drive you this time!" As bad as the week was, it was a lesson in asking for help, something that is hard for so many of us. Why is that so?

Meantime, there was at least one funny moment (and a few misunderstandings) among all the little fiascos last week. The first *malentendu* happened when Mom showed up at the house, ready for our ride to the clinic. After she had carefully washed from head to toe with iodine for her clinic visit, I was surprised to see her wearing the mink hat she had unearthed at a charity shop a few years ago.

"Mom, you'll need to take off that hat," I said, remembering that only sterile clothes could be worn after the special antiseptic shower.

"Well, I didn't know my hat was controversial!" came Mom's response.

"Oh, Mom!" I sighed, growing increasingly agitated.

It wasn't until two weeks later that I understood Mom's words. It was a simple misunderstanding between us (she thought I was judging her fur hat, while my only concern was the iodine bath!). I wish, instead of getting mad, I had simply asked Mom, "What do you mean by that?"

Onto misunderstandings number two and three…

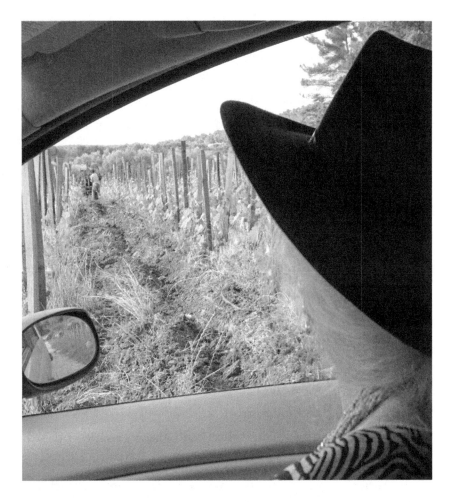

Back in Marseille, arriving for Mom's eye appointment, I was slow-ing down in time to look for a parking spot when the guy behind me began blaring his horn. It's been a while since I've experienced *la fureur routière*, or road rage, given I don't drive often. I cannot share with you here the string of four-letter words he hurled at me, this after an already nerve-racking drive to Marseille. Finally, I pulled aside, letting *Monsieur Gros Mots* pass. That is when I noticed another patient returning to his car. *Quelle chance!*

"*Excusez-moi, Monsieur. Vous partez?*" I asked the man who was paused at the wall beside his car, his back toward me. He didn't seem to hear me so I got out of my vehicle and began to approach when I recognized his curbed posture. *Oh! Le monsieur fait pipi…*

Discreetly as possible I returned to the car and, for his dignity and my own, peeled off out of sight to the lower parking lot where, lo and behold, I ran into Monsieur Gros Mots again. I studied my *pire ennemi*: a thin man wearing a cap. He had found a parking spot and was now darting into the clinic, late, late for a very important date! I made a mental note to have a word with him in *la salle d'attente*. It might be a very awkward moment but after chauffeuring my precious cargo to her doctor's appointment, only to be raged at, my adrenaline was just ripe enough to give Gros Mots a piece of my mind.

Meantime, Mom pointed out a parking spot under the shade of a mulberry tree, and with great relief our 45-minute *trajet* ended. We made it to Jules' appointment on time.

The doctor, wearing a surgical cap and glasses, seemed pressed. Nevertheless, he was thorough. He hesitated before leading us past a full waiting room, to an office where he had another machine. There he took the time to examine Mom's eyes until he concluded, "I cannot give your mom the eye injection today. She has inflammation in both eyes. *C'est l'uvéite.*"

The eye doctor dictated a note to a colleague before giving me the address of a specialist in Gardanne. All I could think at that moment was, *how am I going to drive there, given the morning's stressful voyage*? (Thankfully Jackie and Ana would solve this problem for me later that day.)

On the way home, hesitating at a fork in the road before the freeway entrance I hit a curb and the car lurched. *Ouf!* That was close! I made it onto the freeway and even passed a few semi-trucks. It wasn't until later that evening that I saw the flat tire and realized our good fortune after Mom and I didn't have our tire blow up!

There was a lot to be thankful for including the experienced eye doctor who had taken his time with Mom. Sixty-something with a wiry build and longish salt and pepper hair, it suddenly dawned on me: the doctor looked just like Monsieur Gros Mots back at the parking lot….

No! He couldn't be! I thought, of the potential ironic twist in our morning adventure. Then again both men were pressed and in a hurry… Could it be that Gros Mots was the eye doctor who was late for the afternoon shift? The thought of a villain-turned-virtuous amused me to no end. Well, speaking of endings, *tout est bien qui finit bien!* All's well that ends well. We had a caring doctor (no matter who he might have been before he walked into that office). It all goes to show it is never too late to put your best foot forward, *de faire de son mieux.*

Update: Ana drove us to the appointment at the specialist's in Gardanne, where Mom received some bad news. It is a severe case of bilateral uveitis and she'll need to go to the hospital in Marseille for more tests and possibly some antibiotics to treat an infection. Please keep Jules in your thoughts and prayers. And thanks to our angel driver Ana, who offered to drive us to Marseille for an afternoon of testing, this Tuesday, for Mom.

FRENCH VOCABULARY

jamais deux sans trois
bad things come in threes

la serrure
lock

le frigo
fridge

quel miracle
what a miracle

le pneu crevé
flat tire

le dépanne crevaison
aerosol tire repair and inflator

la bagnole
car (in informal French)

le rendez-vous
appointment

l'autoroute (f)
freeway

le malentendu
misunderstanding

la fureur routière
road rage

quelle chance!
what luck!

Excusez-moi, Monsieur. Vous partez?
Excuse me, Sir. Are you leaving?

faire pipi
to pee

Monsieur Gros Mots
Mr. Foul Mouth

le pire ennemi
worst enemy

la salle d'attente
waiting room

le trajet
trip, journey

l'uvéite (f)
uveitis (inflammation of the uvea, the middle layer of the eye)

ouf!
whew!

tout est bien qui finit bien!
all's well that ends well

faire de son mieux
to put your best foot forward

14

IL DEVAIT EN ÊTRE AINSI

hile French greeting cards are interesting and exotic for family back home, I wanted to celebrate my nephew Payne's college graduation in plain English and was delighted to find a clever card on Amazon France. But, when I received an email informing me I was absent for the delivery and would have to drive to the next town to retrieve my paper-thin parcel (the card would've easily fit in my mailbox), that delight turned to *dégoût*. "But we were home all day!" I grumbled to my dog, Ricci. "I'll bet the driver took the easy route, dropping it with a lot of other packages at the nearest (for him) *dépôt*!"

While I had a mind to report the rogue *livreur*, intuition whispered to go with the flow of what Life (if not the driver) had successfully delivered: an opportunity to put my current *soucis* on hold and get out for some fresh air and *flânerie*. At the very least, it would be the chance to practice my driving, which is rusty after all these years of being a passenger.

The Mistral wind in full force, our compact Renault Zoe swayed back and forth along the road to Ceyreste but I made it

safely to the village and even found parking. What a pleasure to see the vintage Tabac sign near the church square had not been taken down, and ditto for a few other old businesses including Boucherie Jacky. I would have liked to explore more but the wind was sending my hair flying in every direction and I just wanted to get my nephew's card and go home to my warm bed for *une sieste* with my dog.

I don't know what it's like *chez vous*, but in France packages that cannot be delivered to a home address are rerouted to a *point relais*. It's a good way to discover and support a variety of local shops, who go to the trouble of handling the parcels. I once collected a dog leash at a cannabis shop and *une couette* at a former garage turned optical. For my nephew's *carte de vœux* the packet has ended up at a *primeur* of all places.

The greengrocer's was easy to find. I could see the colorful produce a block away. Entering the shop, there was a customer before me, so I moseyed on over to the root vegetables and selected a bunch of carrots (for a fresh *jus de carotte* for Jules every morning to help her eyes). While filling my basket I overheard the shopkeeper talking to the older gentleman:

"I'm afraid we don't carry *fougasse* here, Jean-Pierre," she said gently. "You might try the baker."

Monsieur looked confused. After a long pause he asked for *du lait*.

"Sorry, Jean-Pierre. No milk here; we sell fruits and vegetables." With that, the shopkeeper shot a conspiratorial wink my way. "But I can offer you a coffee. The machine's in the back."

"Do you have sugar?" came the hopeful response.

"No, I don't have sugar...."

Monsieur looked over at me as if I might be able to produce a few cubes from thin air. "It's not bad without sugar," I smiled. "*C'est mieux pour la santé.*"

"*Vous savez, j'ai travaillé dans le nucléaire.*" You know, I worked in the nuclear industry, Monsieur offered, out of the blue.

I gathered he meant, 'What does sugar matter when you've worked around radiation?' but he was only reminiscing. "I lived in Avignon…and Qatar…and Algeria….(He mentioned a few other cities but I lost track, focusing instead on his innocent eyes, the color of *la noisette* he would now be drinking if only there was milk in this fruits and vegetables-only shop.)

"What was your favorite place?" I set down my basket to listen closely.

"*L'Algérie. Oui, L'Algérie…*"

"I hear it is beautiful there," I said.

As the venerable *Ceyresten* struggled to convey the beauty of North Africa to his captive audience of two, I experienced that rare sensation of time standing still. In that moment, there was no rush, no rigid routine, and no pressure to produce (though there was plenty of produce, green and leafy, surrounding us). When he finished speaking, I reached over and placed my hand on Monsieur's shoulder, without stopping to think about cultural norms or boundaries.

"That's lovely. Thank you, Jean-Pierre. Did your sister send you out for anything else?" The shopkeeper smiled, jogging Monsieur's memory.

"Perhaps," he said, thinking about it. During the pause, the shopkeeper gestured towards me and I handed over a basket full of carrots. "Oh, I have something to pick up as well. I don't know why a little greeting card I ordered was delivered here," I shared.

The shopkeeper sympathized, "Maybe it was meant to be."

Driving home I thought about the errant postman, who wasn't such a bad guy after all. Now, looking at the bigger picture, I see his role as some kind of cosmic carrier, rerouting my own, and a few others' paths that day…and also the role of the tiny parcel, in altering our schedules and so tinkering with Father Time. Perhaps that is peace: when the clock stops ticking and the heart opens up to the moment at hand.

I can't end this update without sharing the message on my nephew's graduation card: (First, picture a dachshund wearing a party hat): "Well done you clever sausage!" the card reads. Today, this message also applies to my Mom, for her cheery, positive, and grateful attitude while being poked and prodded at *Hôpital Européen* in Marseille on Tuesday. As we keep Jules in our thoughts and prayers, her French health insurance is set to expire this week. We eagerly await its renewal, crucial for her upcoming 4-day hospital stay and a battery of tests aimed at uncovering the cause of her inflammation.

FRENCH VOCABULARY

Il devait en être ainsi
It was meant to be

le changement de propriétaire
change of owner

le dégoût
strong disappointment

le dépôt
drop-off site

le livreur, la livreuse
delivery man, delivery woman

le souci
worry

la flânerie
stroll, ramble

la sieste
siesta, nap

chez vous
where you're from

le point relais
parcel pickup location

la couette
duvet, comforter

la carte de voeux
greetings card

le primeur
greengrocer

le jus de carotte
carrot juice

la fougasse
the French equivalent of focaccia bread

le lait
milk

une noisette
"a hazelnut" means a shot of coffee with milk in a very small cup

c'est mieux pour la santé
it's healthier

j'ai travaillé dans le nucléaire
I worked in nuclear

MAY

Mai

15

VOIR LA VIE EN ROSE

The weather report was wrong. Fortunately, it wasn't pouring down rain, but there were other traveling *ennuis* when we drove Mom to the hospital for her eye condition. Coming out of Marseille's *Prado Carénage* tunnel, my daughter blared her horn. *"Mais ils conduisent comme des fous!"* she gasped, as the car to our right cut over, causing us to swerve. "You would have never been able to drive here, Mom!"

"Don't say that, Jackie! It's discouraging. I'm sure I could've driven. I memorized the map all week," I argued, from the copilot seat. Currently, we were arriving at "that building with the arched windows", and it was just as Google depicted it. "Turn left at the BMW dealership, Jackie!" There it was, exactly as the online photo in Google Maps indicated.

"You're a great driver, Jackie!" Jules cheered from the back. You'd never know from her words that Mom was uneasy. By focusing on the positive, she was now a voyager on an exciting ride, instead of petrified. Listening to our passenger, I'm reminded of a title Mom kept on the bookshelf when my sister and I were growing up. Flor-

ence Scovel Schinn's *Your Word is Your Wand* was eventually replaced by The Holy Bible which we call "The Living Word." I find the French translation fascinating: *The Word*, which is considered alive and active appears as "*Le Verbe*" in certain editions. "In the beginning was The Word...*Au commencement était le Verbe...*" (*Jean 1:1*)

Words and vision have always been important to Mom. One of the first lessons Mom taught my sister and me was to see things that are not as though they were. Though it was hard for me to see all the D's on my report card as A's, or to view my crooked teeth as straight, Mom's scripture-based wisdom proved itself in the end—with the help of long hours of study and braces. (*Aide-toi, le ciel t'aidera!*)

But back to our narrative in which Mom's faith-filled eyes are, ironically, suffering from inflammation. The doctor's assistant had already warned me that the European Hospital was in a not-so-safe part of Marseille (I guess BMW thinks as positively as Mom…). Outside our car windows, I saw boarded-up businesses and an automobile repair shop covered in graffiti, a lone pair of jeans dangling on a clothesline above. But from Mom's perspective, you'd think we were in a charming French village and not the gritty city. "I love it here. I've always loved Marseille!"

"Mom, hold on to my arm!" I urged, after Jackie pulled in front of *L'Hôpital Européen* to drop us off. "What a beautiful hospital!" Jules enthused. Looking around, I saw patients walking with mobile IV drip bags, others in wheelchairs, and some with canes. All looked pale, but to Mom, they were nearly sunkissed.

Mom winked at the giant security guard at the entrance. Meanwhile, I saw the *agent de protection* differently and began to envision a band of thugs hurrying past us on their way to ER following another *règlement de compte*.

"Did you see those handsome men pushing the wheelchairs?" Mom said, pointing to the *aides-soignants*. "When I check in next month I'll have them race me down the halls and across the street for a glass of wine at that darling café!" To Mom, even the nearby *commerces* (including *les pompes funèbres*, or funeral parlor) appeared otherly.

Having cleared security, now on our way to the first appointment in section C1 of the hospital, Mom's enthusiasm ramped up, perhaps along with her anxiety. "This place looks like a resort!" This sunny outlook was beginning to affect me, and I could now begin to see the clean, modern lines of the great hall which reminded me of a shopping mall. In fact, we were very close to the popular *Les Terrasses du Port* shopping center, where Jackie had gone after dropping us off. Why not see this place as a little extension of that? Therefore, Mom and I were only in one of the "department stores."

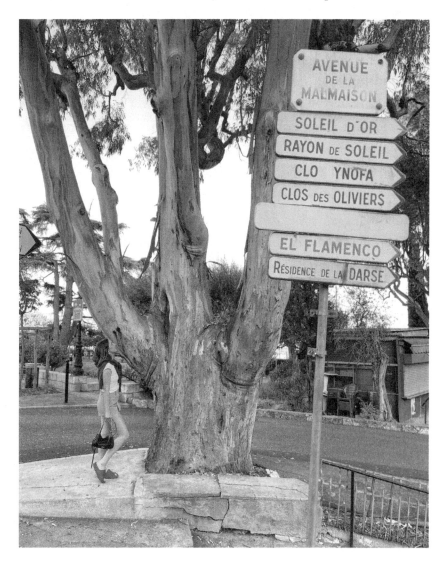

In the hospital's ophthalmology unit, I pulled a number from the ticket dispenser, ushered Mom to a seat, and began rifling through my bag for administrative forms, for Mom's American passport, her prescriptions—all the while translating any instructions to Mom in English or to the healthcare workers in French. While Mom found each *étape* amusing, I sweated them all. The receptionist called our number and fell instantly under Mom's charm, as I sighed a breath of relief (*Ouf!* Mom's insurance card passed inspection).

We were in the second waiting room when Mom's doctor appeared with a bottle of eye drops to dilate her eyes. "*Enlevez votre chapeau, s'il vous plaît,*" the doctor said, to which Mom removed her well-worn Panama hat—but not without a little reluctance. Her trademark *chapeau* is a little like her shield. I held my breath, wondering, *would all of her positivity disappear now?*

When next I looked over, Mom was smiling demurely. I could see she was smitten by the doctor! It was at this point that I knew Mom would get through this current trial. If there's one thing in the world that trumps positive thinking, *it's love!*

And I knew, by the grace from above, I'd get through it too, no matter how many times I stumble as a caregiver.

Standing outside on the gritty curb, waiting for Jackie to pick us up, Mom was filled with gratitude, even as the *Mistral* threatened to carry off her hat. As she held on tight to her Panama and to me, she beamed. "I'm so proud of you," she said. "I'll bet these doctors are impressed with how organized you were!"

Well, I wouldn't go that far! But then…*Il faut voir les choses qui ne sont pas comme si elles l'étaient.*

FRENCH VOCABULARY

voir la vie en rose
to see life through
rose-tinted glasses

l'ennui
problem,
aggravating factor

**Mais ils
conduisent comme
des fous!**
But they drive like
crazy people!

**Le Verbe
(Parole de Dieu)**
The Word
(Word of God)

**Au commence-
ment était Le
Verbe (Jean 1:1)**
In the beginning
was the Word
(John 1:1)

**L'Hôpital
Européen**
The European
Hospital

**Aide-toi, le ciel
t'aidera!**
God helps those
who help themselves

**l'agent
de protection**
security guard

**le règlement
de compte**
settling of scores

**l'aide-soignant (m),
l'aide-soignante (f)**
nurse's aide

le commerce
business

**les pompes
funèbres**
funeral parlor

une étape
step

ouf
phew!

**Enlevez votre
chapeau, s'il vous
plaît**
take off your hat,
please

le Mistral
a strong cold dry
northerly wind of
southern France

**Voir les choses qui
ne sont pas comme
si elles l'étaient**
See things that
are not as though
they were.

*(Note: Romans 4:17—
encourages seeing potential
outcomes as if they are
already real.)*

16
TROUVAILLE

There was a time, years ago, when I might have sold my soul for my garden. I remember that exact moment, kneeling beside a rock bed overflowing with parsley and strawberries and buzzing with life in December. The sweet-scented earth, the vivid colors, the warm sun on my back, a ladybug alighting in the midst of it all. This was heaven on earth. Suddenly, I had the thought that I never want to die and so be separated from this terrestrial paradise. I wrote about the experience in our story, *The Lost Gardens: A Story of Two Vineyards and a Marriage* (there, you know how that ended).

By now you may be picturing a magnificent floral kingdom, but a beautiful garden is subjective, isn't it? One person pictures a stately *Jardin de Versailles*, while another envisions a charming potager. My own digs were a messy affair: wild, expansive, out of control. A marriage of weeds and peas and bees and sore knees. Artichokes spread from the garden beds up through the thyme-scented hillside where my husband had begun to carve out his "vineyard in the sky." There, midway up the hill to heaven, I had strawberries galore and exotic berries–tangy *argousiers*. It was a permaculture playground just as I had imagined it could be. What pride and joy I felt collecting the first (and what would be the last…) creamy, perfectly ripe avocado. Soon after, the *avocatier* was taken over by an army of bugs–and that, in a nutshell, is the story of my garden: a tale of victories and defeats.

Among all the love and war in the garden were the unending *trouvailles*—the discoveries! When I stop to think about it, what gave me the most joy wasn't the way my garden looked or what it produced, no—all the pleasure and excitement came from the surprises it offered up, *les petites merveilles* meted out according to its mysterious whims. At Mas des Brun, where we lived for 5 years, those surprises were the fruits, vegetables, and flowers popping up all over the field. While here in La Ciotat, in a crowded neighborhood where we moved after selling our vineyard, there are other hidden treasures to keep me tied to the garden even if this particular yard, made of sand and clay, has been nothing but a struggle.

I'll never forget the first thrilling discovery this urban lot offered up. Soon after we arrived in 2017, relaxing back into *une chaise longue* beside the fountain/pond, I looked up to a branch laden with green plums. *Mon Dieu!* A second prune tree mixed in among *les haies*! And, speaking of hedges, soon after Mom moved here, to a converted garage on the northwest corner of the house, she discovered a family of hedgehogs—*les hérissons*. Wildlife in the city!

Following on the heels of those hogs, three *arbres de Judée* revealed themselves by springtime (hard to continue hiding among the green hedges with so many fuchsia flowers popping up on your branches). Below, dozens of *coquelicots* appeared across the yard, and the surprises only continued. There was little room to mourn the loss of my permaculture garden, what with so many *nouveautés*

springing up across this stubborn plot. After wrestling with this garden for seven years, this springtime has seen the most blossoms. I like to think the return of a dog to the property has influenced its fertility somehow, some way. (All those joyous four-pawed romps around the garden may have stirred the seeds below. Thanks, Ricci, and rest in peace, dear Smokey. You will forever be a part of our garden, your ashes resting beneath the *Lilas d'Espagne*, which have spread in abundance, like a dog's love.)

Recently, while playing with Ricci, I spied an Acanthus about to bloom! I hurried over to Mom's to report it, before dragging her out to see it for herself. "Wait, Mom! While you're here, I have another surprise for you…"

Each night this past month, while taking Ricci out for her last run around the garden, my ears were delighted by frog calls. But when I approached the fountain/pond, *la grenouille* was nowhere to be found. Turning to go back into the house, it would croak again, sending me running back to the fountain, searching for the green giant (from the sound of its voice it must've been huge—*un crapaud*!). We played *Cache-Cache* for weeks until, one day, I heard a warble from the tree trunk beside the fountain/pond. Hmmm. A frog in a tree? I studied the would-be refuge, a felled palm tree we'd made into an outdoor table. Currently, the table was speaking to me:

Ribbit…ribbit…ribbit…

I fumbled for my phone's flashlight. Shining it under the table-top, I could not believe my eyes: all those thundering ribbits echoing through our neighborhood were coming not from a bull-frog, but from *une rainette*—a tree frog no bigger than a *macaron*.

As I marvel at how such a tiny creature could add such a powerful blast of character to our garden I am reminded, once again, that it isn't the size or shape or appearance of a garden that brings joy. It is the little findings within it that offer eternal bliss. No need to sell one's soul for this. It is already a gift.

Petite Astuce: If you ever find yourself fretting about the untidiness of your garden—or your living space, for that matter—remember this amusing French saying. '*La bave du crapaud n'atteint pas la blanche colombe*' translates to 'The toad's spit doesn't reach the white dove,' meaning that criticism or negativity can't harm those who remain unaffected by it. So, embrace your garden just as it is, and live life on your own terms.

FRENCH VOCABULARY

la trouvaille
find, discovery

le jardin
garden

le potager
vegetable garden

l'argousier
sea buckthorn berry

l'avocatier (m)
avocado tree

la petite merveille
little marvel

une chaise longue
lawn chair

Mon Dieu!
my goodness!

la haie
hedge

l'hérisson
hedge-hog

l'arbre de Judée
Judas tree

le coquelicot
poppy

la nouveauté
novelty

le Lilas d'Espagne
red valerian

la grenouille
frog

le crapaud
giant toad

le cache-cache
hide-and-seek

une rainette
tree frog

un macaron
macaron
(a small, round
French pastry made
of almond flour and
filled with cream)

une petite astuce
a little tip

**La bave du
crapaud n'atteint
pas la blanche
colombe**
The toad's spit
doesn't reach the
white dove
(or "Sticks and
stones may break
my bones but words
will never hurt me")

17
BANDEROLE

On the eve of American Mother's Day (which differs from *La Fête des Mères* here in France if only by the date) our matriarch Jules was up all night, busy contemplating the sky. Lying in her cozy bed, gazing out *la baie vitrée* beyond the pine trees to a patch of sky blanketing our sleepy seaside town, Mom was guessing the exact celestial location of her *beau-fils*, who, after 3 months away, was en route from New Zealand to France.

"I didn't sleep all night!" Mom said, excited to see her "Number 1 Son" as she calls him. It was rare for Mom to appear on my doorstep before noon, but this was not a normal day. "What time will he be here?!" Jules pressed.

"Mom! I've told you many times. Jean-Marc touches down in Marseille at 10:15 a.m. By the time he goes through immigration, collects his bags, clears customs, and meets Max for the drive home, it will be noon."

"Grandma, I need your help with the Welcome Home banner," Jackie said, diverting her *grand-mère's* attention. It was my daughter's idea to create *une banderole*, but we didn't have many craft supplies and we were running out of time. Shouldn't we put our energy into something more reasonable—like making dessert for our reunion lunch?

"Oh, Mom. Come on! We'll figure it out. Where are the felt tip pens?"

"They're upstairs," I relented. "I'll get them…."

Motion has a way of stirring creative thought and by the time I reached the top of the stairs, boom! It hit me. A roll of wax paper. *Ça fera l'affaire!* Returning with the pens, I grabbed some *papier de cuisson* from the drawer beneath the microwave and unrolled 4 feet of wax paper.

"Will you write the sign?" Jackie asked.

"But you are the one with the pretty handwriting!" Realizing this was no time to dawdle, I accepted the honor and sketched the words "Welcome Home" in all caps before grandmother and granddaughter went to work decorating *l'affiche*. Jackie drew the mountains Jean-Marc had climbed (Taranaki and Tongariro) on one side and, in the center, she doodled a partial world map joining France and New Zealand via a dotted line with an airplane flying midway along *les points*.

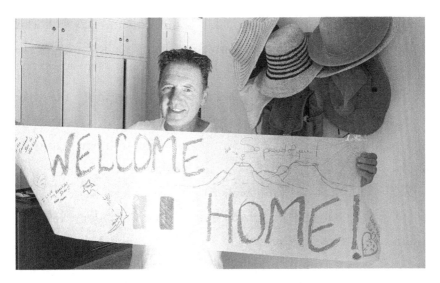

Jules, who normally paints scenes using her palette knife, paused for several moments holding a foreign object in her hand: a Sharpie. To Mom, a pen was something you wrote with; nevertheless, she painted, this time, with words:

"Jean-Marc is the Greatest Son in the World!" she exclaimed, in one stroke, and "I love my beautiful son!! XOXO Mom" in another. A final flourish read, simply "I love you" (enclosed in a pink heart).

A bright yellow orb shone from the right side of *la banderole*. Beside le soleil the words SO PROUD OF YOU! summed up our collective message. Finally, to the lower right, I carved out an old-fashioned heart with our initials JM + K. Voilà our heartfelt banner–and there I'd thought it would be a complicated project. Sometimes you've got to trust in *la spontanéité*. Speaking of which…the queen of spontaneity had an idea:

"Here, take my credit card and go buy some of those little *patisseries* at the baker!" Just like that, Jules had graciously solved our dessert dilemma. Meantime, Jackie could not find any balloons but located some sparklers and attached them to a bottle of rosé to be carried out as the family sang *Bienvenue, Papa!*

We had just pulled everything together, including the cake run, when we heard voices in the garden—and those weren't the neighborhood cats. Max came in first, in time to hurry over to *la banderole* and add a final message for his dad: it read "*Vigneron du monde!*" (Worldwide Wine Maker!) *En effet*, if Jean-Marc had left for New Zealand in the first place, it was for more than climbing mountains, he was there to help a team of winemakers as well as to reach new summits in his own wine path: he even managed to make 50 liters of rosé on the side. (Unfortunately, there was too much sugar in the grapes or this would have been his fifth batch of Ephemera—a series of ephemeral wines he makes now and then from various locations: Willamette Valley, OR, USA; Etna, Sicily, Italy; and Provence, France).

His own ephemeral journey over, here he was now, in the flesh, our Chief Grape! He had dropped 4 kilos but that mischievous grin was bigger than ever as he stood there on the threshold of our home. Ricci ran up, and we all held our collective breath. Would she recognize the disheveled voyager? After all, we had adopted her before Jean-Marc left for New Zealand.

Our little shepherd approached cautiously until a warm recognition came over her. *Ça y est. Son maitre était de retour!* With that, the room erupted in cheers:

"*Bienvenue, Papa!*"

"*Papouche!!*"

"Welcome home, *Chérito!*"

"There's my son!"

"Woof! woof!"

Jean-Marc's eyes glassed over as he hugged each of us, deeply touched by the warm welcome. "*Merci pour ce chaleureux accueil. Merci, merci, c'est gentil,*" he repeated, his voice full of emotion. In the distance, the colorful banner added extra cheer, reminding me of the spontaneous joy that comes from following a loving hunch. Bravo, Jackie, for the symbolic *banderole*. It will be a tradition from here on out, wax paper and all!

POST NOTE: After the heartfelt reunion everyone ran to the beach to jump into the sea—everyone, except Grandma, Ricci, and me. As my husband often reminds me, "Just do what you want to do!" *Chacun fait ce qu'il a envie de faire!* I leave you with that little bit of Chief Grape wisdom, along with a touch of my own (learned from a French grammar teacher in college): "There are exceptions to every rule." Do what you want to do—go to the party or don't if you don't want to, but know when you must go.

This is how my husband and I were able to give each other the freedom to pursue our personal interests these past three months. He climbed mountains, and I dove deep into my own challenging and rewarding pursuits, including writing and caring for my Mom. This together-apart fusion reminds me of the words of Antoine de Saint-Exupéry:

"*Aimer, ce n'est pas se regarder l'un l'autre, c'est regarder ensemble dans la même direction.*" *Love is not just looking at each other, it's looking in the same direction.*

FRENCH VOCABULARY

La Fête des Mères
Mother's Day

la baie vitrée
bay window

le beau-fils
son-in-law

en route
on the way

la grand-mère
grandmother

une banderole
a banner

Ça fera l'affaire
That will do the trick

le papier de cuisson
wax paper

l'affiche
the poster

les points
the points (the dots)

le soleil
the sun

voilà
there you have it

la spontanéité
spontaneity

les pâtisseries
pastries

la bienvenue
the welcome

Vigneron du monde
Worldwide Wine
Maker

en effet
indeed, in fact

Ça y est
There it is

**Son maître était
de retour**
Her master was back

Papouche
a term of
endearment Jackie
uses for her father

Chérito
a term of
endearment,
similar to "dear"
or "darling"

le chaleureux accueil
warm welcome

c'est gentil
that's nice

**Chacun fait
ce qu'il a envie
de faire**
Everyone does what
they want to do

**Antoine de
Saint-Exupéry**
French aviator and
writer (author of,
among others,
Le Petit Prince)

**Aimer, ce n'est pas
se regarder
l'un l'autre,
c'est regarder
ensemble dans la
même direction**
Love is not just
looking at each other,
it's looking in the
same direction

18
CONVOQUER

*F*riday was set to be a joyous celebration of our son's 29th birthday. Instead, it turned into a poignant reminder of the delicate balance between joy and worry that our family is experiencing lately.

Before we left for dinner in Cassis, Max went around the yard to his grandmother's studio in a last-ditch effort to get Jules to join us for the festivities. "What a beautiful dress," Max said, pointing to the panther robe my sister and I had gifted Mom. It was hung on the rack above the kitchen island, beside her bed, where I had begun packing her bag for the hospital.

"Would you try it on for me?" Max persisted. Beyond, two of Mom's doves, Mama and Papa, perched on the bars of her kitchen window, as if waiting for her reply. Talk about lucky ducks: six years ago, when Mom moved in with us and found them in our back yard, it was like winning the bird lottery for those hungry *tourterelles*! The three of them were fast friends and would sit in the garden all day long, the birds landing on Mom's head, her arms, her legs, while Mom fed them sunflower seeds. But, for the past two years, Mom has not spent much time outside, as she has been drawn to her bed, fatigued. So the birds watch over her now from afar, and hurry round the yard to my place when they need food.

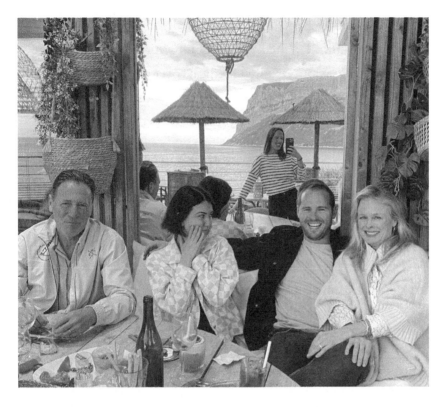

Back in the studio, Mom stood beside Max, hesitant to answer his question. I could tell she was too tired for an impromptu fashion show, yet her eyes lit up. Anything for her darling grandson.

After helping Jules put the robe on over her nightgown, Max stood back in awe. "You look beautiful, Grandma! Won't you come with us tonight? We are going to the hotel in Cassis where Jackie is bartending tonight. Ana will be there, too! And we'll have a beautiful table overlooking the sea!"

"Oh, that sounds wonderful, Max. Another time," Mom smiled, pinching his arm affectionately. She needed to rest, and the stress of waiting to know whether she would be able to go to the hospital, to undergo several exams, was beginning to take a toll.

Last month, after the doctor scheduled Mom's four-day hospital stay for May 20th, I waited anxiously for a message from insurance alerting me that Mom's expired medical coverage had been renewed. Each day, I checked our mailbox twice, sometimes three times. Meanwhile, I waited for the hospital to call to confirm the date.

When May rolled around and still no news from insurance, it dawned on me that, here in France, it was the month of *jours fériés*. With all the national holidays, would Mom's file ever be processed? Finally, on Tuesday, a letter arrived informing me that her *dossier* was incomplete. But how could that be? I had carefully included each item on their checklist! What's more, they were now asking for four additional documents, all of which would be impossible for me to furnish on time (or any time for that matter!).

C'était la panique! But there was no time to clam up. Better to reach out. Ask for help!

Jean-Marc got on the phone, explaining the situation, and, miracle of miracles, *le fonctionnaire* on the other end admitted the setback was their fault and that our dossier was indeed complete. Only, he would now have to send it to another office for validation.

"But this could take weeks!" I cried to Jean-Marc.

"There's nothing we can do but wait," my husband shrugged.

But we didn't have time to wait. May 20th was only six days away!

I tried contacting the hospital to inform them of the situation—that, *malheureusement*, we would need to cancel (if indeed they were still expecting Mom. It seemed more likely she had fallen through the cracks, completely forgotten). I began to wonder if it was worth it to keep calling when, even if I did get through (instead of being rerouted each time and automatically disconnected), it meant losing our appointment and therefore losing contact with the hospital's internist—in which case Mom would really be set back.

Then, on Friday, I was surprised by a brief message on my answering machine: "*Vous êtes convoquée à l'hôpital lundi à 15 heures.*"

Wait. What? At the eleventh hour, the hospital calls to confirm? This posed yet another *souci*: I needed to warn them we wouldn't be showing up! Not without insurance! As I struggled to know just what to do next, I kept hearing the nurse's authoritative voice replay in my head:

"*Vous êtes convoquée à l'hôpital lundi à 15 heures.*"

We were being convoked. Well, in that case, why not simply follow orders? Why complicate things? Just follow the plan and trust everything will work out. These thoughts were immediately freeing, and my anxieties began to fall away, finally.

These past three weeks have been especially nerve-racking, with Mom getting worse by the day. Apart from making her as comfortable as possible, I feel so helpless. I burst into tears at the most unexpected times and in inappropriate places—much like a friend of ours who lost her son, only the loved one I'm grieving is still with me. But for how long? How serious is Mom's condition? It began with a sharp pain behind her eye, which eventually was diagnosed as inflammation…uveitis. But there was something beneath even this, the doctor explained, suspecting some sort of autoimmune issue.

Watching Mom grow more and more tired by the day, and after the disheartening news from insurance, I could not wait one more minute for word from them confirming her coverage. I called my sister Heidi and it was easily decided: Mom would go into the hospital on Monday! We would stick to the plan. She would undergo testing, with or without *l'assurance française*! From here on out we would depend on the holy assurance from above and from within: the conviction that if Mom needed to go to the hospital, *she would go*!

Now that our decision has been made, I feel relief mixed with fear. But more relief than fear. This is a leap of faith and, come what may, we will continue to trust that everything will work out. Sometimes, all we can do is trust in the process and hold on to hope. *Tout va bien se passer.* And, with all hope, Mom will be feeling better soon. Given her positive, grateful, and faithful attitude, she is halfway there! Now, let's get her all of the way through this with a collective prayer: if each person reading this would pause and take a moment to think of Jules, to wish her all good health and healing, I am certain this unified *prière* will begin to work inside every cell in her precious body. And before long, we'll have a second chance to dine in Cassis, with Mom in that smashing panther robe. I can already feel the sea breeze!

FRENCH VOCABULARY

convoquer
to summon

la tourterelle
dove

les jours fériés
public holidays

le dossier
file

la panique
panic

le/la fonctionnaire
the bureaucrat

malheureusement
unfortunately

**Vous êtes
convoquée à
l'hôpital lundi
à 15 heures**
You are summoned
to the hospital on
Monday at 3 PM

le souci
worry, concern

**l'assurance
française**
French insurance

**Tout va bien
se passer**
Everything will
be alright

la prière
prayer

19

BONNE FÊTE MAMAN

Sunday morning, with ten minutes to spare before church, a rack of summer pants caught my eye. A little boutique on *Rue des Poilus* was going out of business, and everything was on sale. It was Mother's Day in France, and although we had already celebrated American Mother's Day two weeks before, I decided to observe it twice this year by offering Mom a nice pair of summer pants. We certainly had something to celebrate: Mom was getting a second lease on life after checking into the hospital last Monday.

Though she asked me not to visit this weekend, I missed Mom terribly. Besides, she needed shampoo, Kleenex, and a fresh towel after a week in the hospital (hospitals in France do not provide these essentials). I decided to surprise her with a brief visit—just 30 minutes. *"Pas plus!"* No more! After all, she had kicked me out a few times and gently told me not to come back over the weekend. I finally understood how exhausting it is to receive visitors, even your own daughter, when you're in a hospital.

Running late now for church, I grabbed a pair of black linen pants from the outdoor rack and hurried inside to pay when a woman *d'un certain âge* appeared at the entrance. *"Coucou!"* she said to the owner, wishing her the best with a wide smile. For as reserved and shy as the boutique owner and I were, Madame was exuberant. Impeccably styled with her hair teased and lacquered, she held a colorful bouquet of peonies and a bright yellow bag labeled "fine Belgian chocolates."

"Elles sont magnifiques!" the owner smiled.

"I bought them for myself—for Mother's Day!" the woman boasted, stepping into the boutique. *"Et oui, les chocolats aussi!"* she grinned.

As I watched her, she reminded me of Mom, just a few years ago. How I longed for her to return to her vibrant, adventurous self. But I knew Jules' fatigue wasn't from a lack of *la joie de vivre*— it was from an undiagnosed health issue the doctors were only now beginning to understand.

Shaking myself out of my reverie, I turned to the lady with the flowers. *"Quelle bonne idée!"* I said, admitting, "My kids haven't called me yet!" It wasn't fair to imply they had forgotten *la Fête des Mères*. I knew that, after church, I'd be returning home to a nice lunch on the terrace with Max and Ana, though Jackie would be at work. The idea I wouldn't see my daughter on Mother's Day saddened me.

The woman with the flowers turned to me, her smile radiating right through me. She shook the bouquet and smiled, *"On n'est jamais mieux servi que par soi-même!"*

Admiring her style with her leopard purse, her slacks/jacket ensemble, and T-shirt *avec des paillettes*, I just had to tell her how cool she was—in an indirect way (*à la française!*) "I love your attitude. And that's such a great phrase. Could you please repeat it?"

"Bien sûr! On n'est jamais mieux servi que par soi-même."

As I struggled to remember it, Madame encouraged me to write it down, waiting patiently for me to open my phone and find my notes. I mouthed the translation as I typed: "If you want to get something done, you have to do it yourself." It was a wonderful lesson from a dynamic woman, who shared she was eighty-five and always looking on the bright side. I couldn't wait to get to the hospital and share the encounter with Mom while she opened her presents (*du coup*, I also got her a box of chocolates and flowers, compliments of my sister Heidi and me).

At the *Hôpital Européen* in Marseille, I knocked quietly on door number 3404. Mom sat up in bed, surprised to see me and Jean-Marc. She looked more beautiful than ever, without makeup and her trademark Panama. *Une beauté naturelle!* "I'm so glad you are here," she admitted, revealing her loneliness. When she reached out to hug us, I saw the bruises up and down her arms. "They're bloodthirsty here," Mom laughed, making light of the many *prises de sang* she had given the nurses.

I noticed Mom no longer had her new favorite pillow—the "*traversin*" she had discovered in her room that first day. She had shared that room with two different patients before being transferred to her own room, in which the *traversin* was forgotten.

"Mom, you've got to speak up. Ask for what you need! By the way, did they ever bring you that bottle of water? And are they giving you your eye drops—three different kinds a day? I hope they are remembering to take your blood pressure from below your knee!" (We learned that, in France, for those who have had breast cancer, protocol is not to take blood pressure from the arm. Something about lymph nodes and swelling.)

Not wanting to wear Mom out with reminders, I delivered the bottom line. "Mom! You know what Grandma Audrey used to say: 'The squeaky wheel gets the grease.' Do you know what that means?"

"It means bitch, bitch, bitch if you need something!"

Now that we were laughing again, I broke the news to her. "You will be here a few more days. I'll be back on Tuesday. In the meantime, you've got to advocate for yourself!"

"If only I could advocate for better food," Mom laughed. "Today's was the first good meal all week. So when I was done eating, I took that little menu included with each meal and flipped it over. On the back, I wrote 'BEST MEAL YET.'"

I hope the chef will understand Mom's English. But if Jules gets desperate enough, she might take Madame Flower's advice and head down to the cafeteria to serve herself. Remember, dear reader, *on n'est jamais mieux servi que par soi-même!*

POST NOTE: Hurrying out of the boutique on my way to church, I rounded the corner and was surprised by a lovely young woman sitting on one of the steps. It was Jackie, waiting in the wings to surprise me with a "Happy Mother's Day, Mom!"

FRENCH VOCABULARY

Bonne Fête, Maman!
Happy Mother's Day, Mom!

l'église (f)
church

le poilu
informal name for a French WWI soldier, literally "hairy" or "shaggy"

La Rue des Poilus
Poilus Street (named in honor of the French WWI soldiers)

les pantalons
pants

elle me manquait
I missed her

Pas plus!
No more!

d'un certain âge
of a certain age

Coucou!
Hi there!

Elles sont magnifiques!
They are magnificent!

Et oui, les chocolats aussi!
And yes, the chocolates too!

la joie de vivre
zest for life

Quelle bonne idée!
What a good idea!

On n'est jamais mieux servi que par soi-même
If you want to get something done, you have to do it yourself

l'ensemble
outfit

avec des paillettes
with sequins

à la française!
in the French way!

Bien sûr!
Of course!

du coup
as a result / so

L'Hôpital Européen (m)
The European Hospital

une beauté naturelle
a natural beauty

la prise de sang
blood sample

le traversin
the bolster pillow

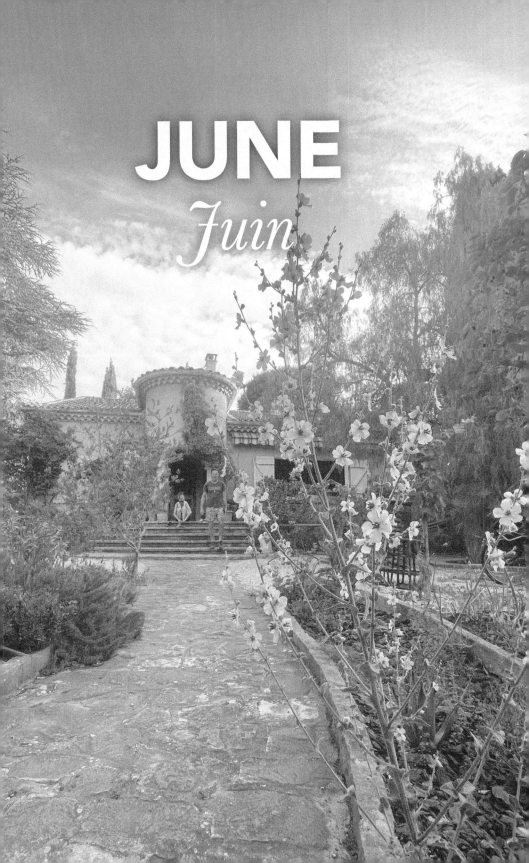

JUNE

Juin

20

LA BELLE AU BOIS DORMANT

I had a dream last night that Mom was driving us in our jeep. We were going up a dirt road, and when we reached *le sommet* and came over the other side, the path dropped unexpectedly into a swamp, along with our *bagnole*!

I remembered, with relief, that our vehicle had 4-wheel drive, that is, until our tires lost contact with the ground and we began to sink.

Just when all hope seemed lost, Mom looked over at me with confidence, revved the engine, and the Jeep swam forward enough for the wheels to catch on the rocks below. *Alléluia*! We climbed right out of the mire! On the other side of the water, there was a farm, and the couple living there had a family of hedgehogs. They kindly gifted us the baby *hérisson*. Not only had we survived, but we surfaced from the mire with a gift—a newborn!

If dreams were premonitions, what a hopeful sign this would be! As it is, we are still bogged down in this mire of medical testing and administrative *imbroglio*. Meanwhile, we had a momentary reprieve from the situation when, on Thursday, Mom's internist released her from the hospital for the weekend.

During her three days at home in her cozy studio, Jules read each and every comment readers have left on my blog following her hospitalization. Mom was filled with energy from your thoughts and prayers and amazed by my extended family of readers, whose affection and care were palpable. I assured Mom I appreciate all of you so much and hope you feel this gratitude in these weekly updates.

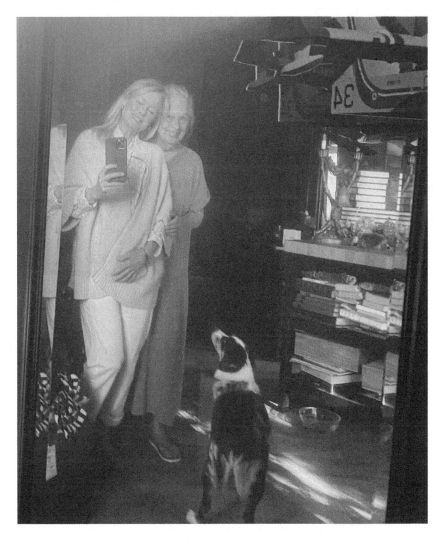

Tucked into her own bed, Ricci cuddled beside her, Mom told me all about the care and attention she's receiving at the hospital. *Les infirmières* have even given Mom *un nom d'affection*: Jules is called "Sleeping Beauty" or "*La Belle Au Bois Dormant*" for the way she sleeps around the clock. This is one reason she went into the hospital—to find out why she is so tired.

For her first PET scan, *La Belle Au Bois Dormant* was transported via stretcher to a tiny room, where she received a catheter in her arm. To take her mind off the needle, I promised Mom that when this was all over, we'd go off on an adventure somewhere.

"Oh, Kristi," Mom began.

I turned to focus on what she was saying, quieting the chatter in my mind that droned on: I need to pick up Mom's medication… It's close to 2pm! I've got to get the car back to Jackie who'll need it for work!

"Kristi, this is an adventure!" Mom smiled. "Aren't you proud of France?!"

Me? Proud of France? But I'm not even French. Can you be proud of something that is not your own? Mom's expectant look had me reflecting. Just what did she mean?

"I cannot believe how dedicated and professional everyone working here is. They all know they have an important job. They are saving lives!" Mom continued.

I took my mom's precious hand into my own. "To this adventure," I said, kissing Mom before they wheeled her into the next room. When the door shut behind her, I saw the number 7. *Mais bien sûr*, of course she would have room number 7. It's her favorite number—*le numéro sacré*. Not only is Mom lucky, but she is truly blessed!

Just before Mom disappeared into the PET scan, she tried to calm my doubts and fears. "How else would we witness God's miracles if it wasn't for these uncertainties?"

For her daughters and those who know her, Jules is proof that faith, like our trusty Jeep, can move us out of the deepest mire. And in this medical care adventure, the gift we surface with is the unwavering love and support from those around us, a reminder that even in challenging times, we are never alone. Not even as a stranger in a foreign land. *Oui, Maman! Je suis fière de la France!*

FRENCH VOCABULARY

La Belle au Bois Dormant
Sleeping Beauty

le sommet
the summit

la bagnole
car
(in informal French)

Alléluia!
Hallelujah!

l'hérisson (m)
hedgehog

l'imbroglio (m)
mess

les infirmières (m/f)
the nurses

le nom d'affection
a term of endearment

mais bien sûr
but of course

le numéro sacré
the holy number

jamais tout seul
(we are) never alone

Oui, Maman
Yes, Mom

Je suis fière de la France!
I am proud of France!

"*Ça gratte!* It itches!" I say to Jean-Marc, waking up with fresh bites on my arm. I can't believe it! They've struck again! But just who are *they* is the question. What, exactly, is biting me every night? My skin is swollen and I see red bumps, *ici et par là*, across my arms, stomach, and legs. It's an exercise in willpower not to scratch them, so I claw at the skin on either side and wake up my husband. *La misère aime la compagnie!*

"Are you sure you haven't been bitten?" I look over at Jean-Marc, who is groggy from sleep.

"*Je n'ai pas de piqûres,*" he mumbles. Well, it can't be bed bugs then, can it? Besides, I would have noticed the intruders, having studied the situation since the famous breakout in Paris last year. *Les punaises* are visible.

Perplexed, I go down the culprit list once again…

Could it be *un moustique qui me pique?* Mosquito season began a few weeks ago but it is unlikely a winged want-not has crawled beneath my covers to bite me on the bottom!

What about *les puces?* Could fleas be eating me? I look around my bed, scrutinizing the sheets, but *les puces* are nowhere to be seen. I'd recognize them, having dealt with the little critters when we brought our dog home from the farm eight months ago. Our

adoptee, Ricci, was covered in the bloodsucking parasites. During the five-hour ride home from Aveyron I squashed as many as I could—proof that fleas are big enough to see.

Et si c'était les araignées? Spiders are common around here, given we don't spray pesticides. Could these be spider bites I'm getting each night?

How about *les mites*? Mites don't bite, Jean-Marc informs me. Maybe dust mites don't bite but other kinds of mites might! Bird mites? Could it be our family of *tourterelles* is sharing more than their good company?

What if it's *un méchant taon*? I saw one flying around my bed just this morning! Could a horrible horsefly be behind these itchy lumps and bumps?

Jean-Marc suggested it might be hives, as they have, coincidentally, come up since my mom went into the hospital. According to Google, "Stress hives can resemble insect bites…" Is it all the nerve-racking driving to Marseille and beyond that's gotten under my skin? Or the agonizing wait for Mom's health insurance to kick in?

Until I know just what's biting me, physically or emotionally, I've sprinkled baking soda across my mattress (Mom says it will dry the suckers out!), changed my sheets, my pajamas, and sprayed lavender mist all over the bedroom after Jean-Marc vacuumed. This relieved things for a few days, but the itchy *boutons* returned!

As I sit here scratching beneath my chin (the most recent *morsure*), I think about another possibility: no-see-ums. The funny term refers to tiny, winged creatures that bite. These gnats are called *moucherons* in French. But Jean-Marc says it can't be them because they can't fly under the covers.

Could it be that all these bites, then, are happening during the day? Are "no-see-ums," finally, to blame? Even if this mystery is close to being solved, the solution to no-see-ums is nowhere in sight. And, frankly, apart from lavender and baking soda, I'm not going to put too much more energy into *cette situation gênante*. No, you won't see me running around swatting at some invisible enemy. Honestly, I've got other cats to whip at the moment. (Leave it to the French to save the day with an amusing idiom: *avoir d'autres chats à fouetter*) In the meantime I have a fine phrasal verb for the pests: BUG OFF! *Va t'en!*

FRENCH VOCABULARY

la piqûre
bite, sting

ça gratte
it itches

ici et par là
here and there

**la misère aime
la compagnie**
misery loves
company

**je n'ai pas
de piqûres**
I don't have
any bites

la punaise de lit
bed bug

**un moustique
qui me pique**
a mosquito
biting me

les puces
fleas

**Et si c'était
les araignées?**
And what if
it's spiders?

les mites
mites

la tourterelle
collared dove

un méchant taon
a mean horsefly

le bouton
bite

une morsure
a bite

les moucherons
no-see-ums
(biting midges)

**une situation
gênante**
annoying situation

**avoir d'autres
chats à fouetter**
to have bigger
fish to fry

va t'en!
bug off!

22
LE BONHEUR

*M*om and I are lounging in the garden. It's late afternoon, or *la fin de l'après-midi* according to the language of Molière. All around us the birds, the trees, and the sweet-scented breeze offer their own poetic expression in a tongue understood by all. It is nature's intoxicating melody, and we are floating in it now.

"Where is everybody?" Mom wonders, surfacing from the bucolic trance.

I take a deep breath. Mom's frequent questions—'What time is it?' 'What day is it?' and 'Where is everyone?'—keep me busy. Perhaps she's exercising my reporting skills? In reality, she's experiencing short-term memory loss, something we're both familiar with. "Let's see…Jean-Marc is in Marseille, giving a wine tasting. Jackie is in Cassis, working, and Max…Max reminded me just this morning, via text, he is in Croatia."

"Croatia? With Ana?" Mom wonders.

"No, with his friends."

Mom sighs peacefully, leading me to understand a restful vacation can be found right here in our front yard. Jules reclines on a *chaise longue* beside the snapdragons and flowering onions, while I sit nearby on a wooden chair next to the fountain. In the water, the first white *nénuphars* are budding and dragonflies hover here and there.

Ricci is doing figure-eights around us, delighted her mother-daughter *meute* has moved outside. From here our little shepherd can wander over to the hedge where she loves to slip under the flimsy fence and visit the neighbors, just like Smokey did. Only, unlike our dearly departed golden retriever, she barks at *les voisins*.

"Ricci! *Reviens*!" With that we go over the drill: "*Ici c'est chez nous et là c'est chez les voisins*." I can almost hear my dog's thoughts: Yes, but the cats are over there. Little does Ricci know her forays next door are only adding insult to injury: for the day we brought Ricci home, 18-year-old Lili The Cat moved back to the neighbor's (where she decamped when the previous owner of our house (who also owned Lili) left, only to return when Smokey passed away two years ago). When we got Ricci last fall, it was *déjà vu*: there was no way Lili was sharing this yard with *un toutou*!

Back here in the garden, beside the fountain, Mom reaches down to pet our proud protector who is leaning against the side of the lawn chair. "She is so soft," Mom coos. "How can a dog be this soft?"

"I don't know," I admit. It boggles the mind. Then again, just about anything boggles the mind when you are seeped this deep in peace. I wonder how I could ever be so worked up, as I was a few times earlier today, over everything and nothing. What does any of it matter in the grand scheme of things, beyond this garden wall? Sinking back into my chair I relax, inhaling jasmine floating over from the flowering vine beside the *bougainvillea*. We need to sit out here more often, I think, turning to gaze at Mom.

Though it is the second week of June, Jules is wearing a light parka and a woolen cap. I'm beginning to understand why she is cold all of the time and it's not because she lived in Mexico all those years. We'll have more information on Tuesday, when we return to see the internist in Marseille for The Final Report. I've driven back and forth to the city so often, Jean-Marc says I could do it *les yeux fermés*. I feel proud about my new road skills even if it scared me driving home in a storm the day I took Mom back to the hospital.

"The weather has been strange," Mom remarks.

"It sure has," I agree.

"Look at that blue sky now!"

Above the pepper tree, I see the doves flying in. *Zut!* I'm all out of bird food. I go and get some bread, breaking off pieces and dropping them beside the geraniums, unaware Mom is studying me from her chair.

As I scatter bread for the birds, she watches me closely. "You are like a little Julie," she remarks, her eyes twinkling with a mix of nostalgia and pride.

"I'm trying to be," I smile. Mom is and will always be my model, no matter how many things we don't agree on, including who should be president or how often to feed the birds (whenever they're around, Mom would argue). More and more I am coming around to Mom's ways.

When I'm done feeding the birds I go over to investigate a curious shape in the pond. With any luck, it's our resident frog! Kneeling down to stir the water, I see it is only a leaf.

"You have not changed," Mom smiles, sharing a razor-sharp memory from my childhood when I would go exploring in the wash (the empty river bed) behind our trailer. I loved returning after the rain, to sit along the bank and search for tadpoles.

Fifty years later we are worlds away from the trailer park, here in the South of France. Whoever would have guessed such a future? I settle back into the chair beside Mom and we sneak glances at each other. These are like little pinches to the arms reminding us how lucky we are to be here, together. A moment of quiet pervades our union in the garden, as the fountain gushes, the perfume of jasmine wafts past, and the soft fur of Ricci, resting between our chairs, caresses our skin. The concerns of the day have disappeared into this peaceful moment. A few more moments float by with only the sounds of nature when Mom's voice gently punctuates the silence.

"Kristi, this is what it's all about."

I savor Mom's profound declaration, internalizing exactly what it means. It is a soulful revelation that, should we think too much about it, might smother us in meaning. Maybe that's why God invented comic relief…

Running my fingers through my hair, my thoughts return to the present. "I can't figure out what's happened to my hair," I say to Mom. "It so stiff and dull! I think I forgot to rinse out the condi-tioner!" I finally admit.

"Welcome to the club!" Mom laughs, acknowledging our shared absentmindedness. And we sink back into our chairs, lighthearted, as the birds, the dragonflies, the dog, the frog, the flowers, and all of the trees carry on effortlessly, oblivious to the time or the date. If only we could live on forever this way, in this carefree garden, free from worries and the march of time.

FRENCH VOCABULARY

le bonheur
happiness

**la fin de
l'après-midi**
late afternoon

la chaise longue
lounge chair

les nénuphars
water lilies

a meute
pack

les voisins
the neighbors

reviens
come back

**ici c'est chez nous
et là c'est chez
les voisins**
this is our place
and that is the
neighbors' place

déjà vu
seen it all before
(in this context)

un toutou
a dog

les yeux fermés
with eyes closed

zut
darn

23

LA MAUVIETTE

*S*ummer. *La saison estivale* has begun and I am up at the crack of dawn, partly because my dog wakes me early, and partly because my body is aching. Oh, *que j'ai mal!*

To soar like a butterfly, to have knees like the bees, or simply not to be sore upon waking… If only arthritis could be poetic. But it isn't, it's pathetic! These are my thoughts as I begin today's edition, attempting to match *la photo du jour* to the theme of our story about aches and pains.

Barely out of bed and already feeling pressed, I considered opting out of this morning's walk with Jean-Marc. Amidst thoughts of laundry, paperwork, meal planning, and a weekly blog deadline, I realized exercise is as much a priority as working. A stroll through my neighborhood will be the key to getting this creaky engine rolling. *De plus*, it will strengthen my bones, calm my mind, and exercise my social skills (I'll take brief interactions while out walking over a cocktail party any day!).

Closing our front door, I stretch my sore legs and notice the stiffness in my lower back. Hopefully, these *douleurs articulaires* will ease with a little warm-up. As I step outside the front gate, the blooming *laurier rose* and vibrant blue plumbago lift my spirits if not my posture (that will take some mindfulness). Orange trumpet vines, roses,

and purple bougainvillea brighten our neighborhood, as seagulls glide by effortlessly. If exercise fails to set me straight, nature will, coloring my thoughts in vivid hues to lighten the mood.

Halfway into our *balade matinale*, I turn to my husband. "I'm going to pick up Mom's meds. I'll catch up to you after." With that, I cross the road while Jean-Marc heads down to *les roches plates* to swim with *les chiens* (we're dog sitting today). Ricci won't like the water, but she is a willing *nageuse*, if only to return quickly to shore once Jean-Marc gently lowers her into the water. Izzy, Ana's beagle, will opt out in favor of playing lifeguard from her perch on one of the rocks above the sea coast.

At the pharmacy, after filling Mom's prescriptions, I hesitate before leaving. "Could you help me with something else?" I ask *la pharmacienne*. "When I wake up in bed, I'm sore from my hip to my knee. The pain radiates from inside my bones so strongly that I have to get up and walk around for the aching to stop. No more sleeping in. *C'est fini la grasse matinée!*"

The pharmacist smiled knowingly. "*C'est l'âge*. What you are experiencing is a mixture of inflammation, hormones, and meno-pause. *Suivez-moi*." The woman in the lab coat led me past knee wraps, canes, and Ensure to a shelf of herbal supplements. I keep thinking that surely, by looking at me, she will realize this is not my category. Only, when I study her face, it looks very much like mine. She's not yet 60 and yet…

"I had the same aches and pains," she confides.

"Had? Do you mean they will go away on their own?"

"*Pas vraiment*. They'll just change places." She points to her elbow, shoulder, and neck. "*Eh, oui*," she sighs. I'm reminded of the daily phone conversations with my older sister, Heidi, who suffered from pain in her arm all last year. "It's just tendonitis," I assured her. (To think it was probably arthritis all along. *La pauvre!*)

My *confidante* hands me a box labeled "Flex Max Articulations" (for *flexibilité, mobilité, confort articulaire*). This magic potion has curcuma, glucosamine sulfate, chondroitine sulfate, collagen, and vitamins C, D, manganese and costs 24,99€.

"Take two a day."

Putting the herbal supplement in my basket, I'm feeling a mixture of hope and regret (if only my sister had these pills!). As for the aches and pains, "*C'est juste l'effet de grandir*," I tell the pharmacist and so convince myself I am only growing up!

"*C'est ça.*" The pharmacist smiles. I take a moment to appreciate her openness and the fact that we are relating to each other beside the stacks of diapers that may very well be a part of our futures. If it ever gets to that point, I'll know who to go to for help: this friendly woman, the same vintage as me, who is going through similar little miseries.

As for *ces petites misères*, I think of those a decade or two, or three, or four older than me. How is everyone out there feeling? Aging is not for sissies! I'm reminded, only I don't know how to share this with the pharmacist, in French. Besides, at only 56, I can't be sure I'm no longer a sissy. In such redoubtable circumstances, it helps to focus on community: aging is the opportunity to move beyond brief social encounters to nourish new friendships. As the pharmacist handed me the supplements, I realized growing older isn't just about aches. It's about forming new connections. Indeed, aging is not for sissies—it's for sisters.

FRENCH VOCABULARY

la mauviette
sissy

la saison estivale
summer season

oh, que j'ai mal
oh, how I ache

la photo du jour
photo of the day

de plus
moreover

**les douleurs
articulaires**
joint pains

le laurier rose
oleander

la balade matinale
morning walk

les roches plates
flat rocks

**la nageuse
(le nageur)**
the swimmer

les chiens
dogs

**la (le)
pharmacien(ne)**
pharmacist

**c'est fini
la grasse matinée**
no more sleeping in

c'est l'âge
it's age

suivez-moi
follow me

pas vraiment
not really

Eh, oui
oh yes

la (le) pauvre
poor thing

la confidante
confidante

la flexibilité
flexibility

la mobilité
mobility

**le confort
articulaire**
joint comfort

**c'est juste l'effet
de grandir**
it's just a fact of
growing up

c'est ça
that's right

ces petites misères
these little miseries

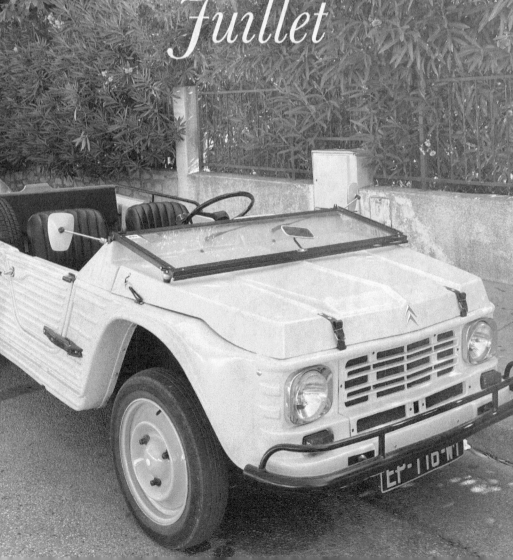

JULY
Juillet

24
LA ROBE
DE MARIÉE

Today is our 30th wedding anniversary! To celebrate this meaningful occasion, Jean-Marc has reserved a table in Marseille, at the beautiful *Calanque de Sormiou*. It's the very place we dined three decades ago, following our civil ceremony. It will be a casual *soirée*, just us and our kidults, but when I found out about our plans I knew I should wear something *soigné*.

Several days ago it occurred to me. What about my wedding dress? Did I still have it and would it fit?

Upstairs in the second *chambre*, I carefully climbed onto a chair and found the wedding dress above our dusty *armoire* in a vintage suitcase. *Quelle chance!* It was wrapped lightly in plastic from the dry cleaners. The cleaning tag was still stapled to the dress's label. Nostalgic, I searched for the cleaning receipt but didn't find it. Google estimates it would have cost 825 French francs (150 dollars back in the day!). I know I would not have paid that much to clean a dress, wedding or otherwise. After all, it wasn't an intricate garment, but a simple flowy-to-the-knees affair. My other, floor-length dress, was reserved for the church ceremony two months later. I see it didn't do as well in storage, considering the large yellow stain on the front. *Quel dommage!*

I carefully slipped the little dress out of its bag, to find it was in good condition, if slightly off-white—but then maybe this was its original color? "Pearly"—fit for a 30th or "pearl anniversary". To think this delicate garment survived eight *déménagements*, amid the heat, the cold, the smoke, the *inondations*, the mold, and any little critters that might have altered its state.

Standing in awe examining my wedding dress of days gone by, I decided to try it on right then and there. To my surprise, it fit (it had the advantage of being an A-line dress, much more forgiving than my church dress, which would no longer button up the back…).

As for this little wedding dress, I now knew I could wear it! I thought to rush down and show my husband, but why not surprise him on our special day? Even if he planned on us arriving a few hours early, to swim in the *calanque*, I could always sit on a rock in the shade and try to stay put together for our nice dinner. Or maybe after all these years I might finally let go, enjoy a swim and then slip into the pretty dress, salty skin and all. No, I don't think I've evolved enough to be this carefree.

Back to the dress… It was full of *plis* from being in the old suitcase. I wondered if I might simply steam out the wrinkles? But what if the heat damages it? You know what they say, "never iron or steam clothing that is soiled." Even if it wasn't dirty, could it be "marked" from time? Did I want to steam in those imagined marks? Why not do as the venerable fashion designer Vivienne Westwood, and never clean your *couture*!

Just leave the dress as is, I decided, no marks, only a few wrinkles. You could treat it as a messy beach cover-up! Then you could go swimming with your hubby. And hold your head high when you arrive for dinner. There, problem solved.

Except that the idea of wearing the dress as it was thirty years ago—new, pristine, and so pretty—would feel amazing on this special day!

Back to square one (or three… Where were we?) It didn't seem right to steam a dress that's been in storage for so long. Alright, I would take it to the dry cleaners. Even if it didn't have "*Le Parfum du Temps*" a cleaning would ensure it had a fresh scent.

Le nettoyage à sec, however, presented further complications. Would it be ready in four days? After all, this is slow France! *Voyons voir*…Let's see… On closer look, the tag inside said the dress was made of polyester. Not exactly a noble fabric, but *un tissu* that can be hand washed as far as I know. Hadn't I handwashed polyester dozens of times? Then again, the tag inside read "dry clean only" … The gentle cycle in my *machine à laver* might be worth the risk, considering I would only be wearing it this one time (I can't see myself unearthing it again for our 60th…then again, why not?). Still, it would be a shame to damage the dress.

Purée! I am beginning to develop decision fatigue. Enough! I'm taking it to the dry cleaners!

Feeling my energy return and, armed with a plan, I left one hour early to tackle what seemed an impossible mission here in France: to get anything done easily, logically, and on time. I am reminded of the time my brother-in-law, Doug, brought seven shirts to the dry cleaners when we lived in St. Maximin and the owner immediately handed back four. It is still a mystery why she refused the rest. "Everything is complicated in France," I explained to my brother-in-law, and from that point on I rarely visited *le pressing* (except to clean our down comforters which don't fit into our tiny washing machine).

Back to my plan of action: with Operation Wedding Dress underway, I would put all chance on my side by getting to the cleaners early. If the first establishment couldn't clean my dress, I had a second place in mind. But I did wonder, even if I found *un pressing* willing and able to clean my dress in 3 days, what would it cost? Looking at my dress, it didn't appear to be a wedding dress. The A-line slip dress could be worn on other occasions, like the popular *Soirée Blanche* the French are so fond of during summertime, where all the guests wear white.

Finally, my guess was 30 euros for the dry cleaning. Just don't tell them it's a wedding dress! Or the cost will double. *Allons-y!*

I collected my keys, ID, a few forms of payment, and the dress, and snuck past my husband. "I'll be back in an hour," I waved. On my way to the car, I said a little prayer. Remember, the Lord is your helper in big things and small. Speaking of small, what if the cleaners shrank my dress?

Putting on my seatbelt, I shook off my doubts and hit the road…and before I knew it, I'd found a parking spot at the busy Carrefour Centre Commercial. I saw the sign for *le pressing* right away. So far so good.

The thin woman at the dry cleaners wore all black and a frown. "*Bonjour,*" I said.

(No reply.)

"*Bonjour, Madame,*" I repeated, remembering protocol. "Just a little question to begin with," I said, sweetly. "Are you able to clean a dress by Thursday?"

"*Montrez-la-moi,*" came the curt response.

Taking the wedding dress out of my *fourre-tout*, I began to describe the situation. When I paused, before continuing on, the woman interrupted:

"That'll be 15 euros."

"You mean it will be ready by Thursday?"

The woman nodded. "Would you like *une carte de fidélité* or is this an exceptional visit?"

"Oh, it's exceptional!" I said, delighted at how simple this complicated process was after all.

I paid 15 euros, thanked the dry cleaner, and headed to my car feeling as light and carefree as a fluttering wedding veil. *Au fait*, maybe I could have dry cleaned my veil too. Oh! I could think of a lot of outfits I could finally take to *le pressing*! On second thought, I should have gotten the loyalty card!

This little adventure just goes to show that maybe France isn't so slow or difficult after all. Perhaps it was my own mindset that needed a little pressing. With my dress now taken care of and our celebration on the horizon, I am eager to begin the second half of this French life—loyalty card in hand. *Joyeux anniversaire, Mon Chéri!*

FRENCH VOCABULARY

la robe de mariée
wedding dress

une calanque
rocky inlet
(specific to the
Mediterranean coast)

une soirée
evening event

soigné
elegant,
well-groomed

une chambre
bedroom

une armoire
wardrobe

quelle chance
what luck

quel dommage
what a pity

un déménagement
move (relocation)

une inondation
flood

un pli
wrinkle

la couture
high-end,
custom-made
clothing

Le Parfum du Temps
The Scent of Time

un nettoyage à sec
dry cleaning

voyons voir
let's see

un tissu
fabric

**une machine
à laver**
washing machine

purée
darn
(mild exclamation)

le pressing
dry cleaner's

la soirée blanche
a party where
everyone wears white

allons-y
let's go

bonjour
hello

bonjour, Madame
hello, ma'am

montrez-la-moi
show it to me

un fourre-tout
tote bag

**une carte
de fidélité**
loyalty card

au fait
by the way

joyeux anniversaire
happy anniversary

**Mon Chéri
(Ma Chérie)**
my dear, my darling

25
POSTCARD
FROM BRITTANY

When we received an invitation for *un mariage* in Brittany, Jean-Marc planned a romantic escapade around this joyous event. We only had three days to vacation together, not counting travel time, but it was enough to mark the occasion of our 30th wedding anniversary. After careful research, my former *fiancé* put together an itinerary including two nights on the island of *Bréhat*, lunch above the beach in *Saint-Sieuc* (back on the mainland), and a half-day in the fortified town of *St. Malo*.

This ambitious *périple* surrounding his godson's wedding filled me with doubts, especially after my husband announced we were limited to one carry-on suitcase. Given we were leaving the heatwave in *La Ciotat* for the rainy north coast—to tromp around a muddy island before heading to a formal affair—packing would be a challenge.

Sacrificing my hairdryer and clothes steamer, I packed two permapress *robes*, a satin *jupe* and *chemise*, two pairs of heels, a raincoat…. (I won't bore you with the rest) and stepped onto our Volotea flight wearing white jeans and a cream-colored blazer that would hopefully go with all three dressy outfits. Wearing half my party attire, I felt somewhat stiffer than usual, especially for a full day of travel, but how else to keep a portion of my wardrobe pressed for the wedding?

As for my no-fuss Frenchman, he carried a lightweight cotton tote (compliments of our local pharmacy), and somehow managed to fit all his needs inside—with room to spare for my umbrella! The bright yellow floral print on his bag was an amusing contrast against his rugged exterior.

The drive to the airport, the plane ride, the rental car, and *la vedette*, went smoothly. However, when we stepped off the ferry boat late that afternoon to find a tractor waiting for us, any embarrassment I felt being the only tourist in white was overcome by panic. How to keep these party clothes clean if we were going to

ride that muddy thing? This being a car-free island, it was ride the tractor or *pédaler*!

Soon enough, another tractor arrived, towing a tiny train. *Ouf!* Boarding one of the train cars, we enjoyed a scenic tour of the island from the *embarcadère* to our friend's house on a bluff above the English Channel, where we would *séjour* for two nights. Arriving at the little stone cottage, the view during high tide was breathtaking as the sun began to set on the orange horizon.

By morning, three little boats in the cove were temporarily stranded among the seagrass and rocks, making for another charming view from the large rock where we would drink our morning coffee and enjoy the evening *apéro* both nights. After a breakfast of *pain au chocolat* and *café crème* in *Le Bourg*, a ten-minute walk from our cottage, Jean-Marc suggested we set out to discover *le phare du Paon* in the northernmost part of the island. But I suddenly felt lazy on learning the distance. It was only four kilometers there and back, but we also had plans to walk to the southernmost end of the island by noon. As I stood there waffling over what to do, the following words tumbled out: *"Je te suis!"*

"I'll follow you!" This new mantra would be my ticket to overcoming indecision, hesitation, and always wanting (if not having) my way. With Jean-Marc in the lead, I was free to photograph the *hortensias* and the hollyhocks (*Bréhat* Island is classified as the "flower island"), the neat stone houses made of local rock, the island dogs, the bikes, the beaches, and coves at high tide and low.

We passed fields with cows, rocky beaches, and curious stone structures. During the peaceful *marche*, Jean-Marc admitted that one thing he loves about these little islands off the coast of Brittany is the feeling of insularity, or safety. Passing an unmanned stand brimming with produce and *confitures*, I understood what he meant. The little stand was packed with homemade jams, vibrant produce and there was even fresh-baked bread. A sign read: *"Petit Marché. Servez-vous et laissez les sous dans la caisse s'il vous plaît."* Serve yourself and leave the money in the cash box.

"This would not go over well in Marseille," I giggled, to which Jean-Marc added, "No, they would take the goods and steal the cash!"

When Jean-Marc suggested lunch on the south coast, I resisted the urge to protest and instead said, *"Je te suis!"* I'm so glad I did. We discovered the island's only sandy beach, *La Plage du Guerzido*, with an inviting terrace shaded by a *parasol* pine. Imagine that! *Un pin parasol!* We marveled at the exotic flora—jasmine, lavender, fig trees, and even pink *tamaris* from the desert—all thriving on this enchanting archipelago.

For our last evening, we enjoyed more local *huitres*, baked *brandade de morue*, and toasted to our full (and only) day on *L'île de Bréhat*, hoping to come back and rent a house and bring the family. (The only risk being rain! We were lucky with our sunny day, but rain is *de rigueur* on this little island along the English Channel. In that case, my family from Seattle would be right at home!)

The next morning we had coffee and *croissants* at Hotel Bellevue on the port before boarding *la vedette* back to the mainland. With time dwindling we hurried to the beach in *Lancieux* for lunch, before heading to our rental to clean up. Only, there were no sheets or towels in our apartment! (It's not uncommon in France to have to bring your own linens.) Undeterred, we used our t-shirts to dry after showering, and made it to the ancient *église* in time to see Julia and Baptiste walk down the aisle. I had to split my Kleenex in two when Jean-Marc's eyes began watering, too! Did he also feel that quiver in his heart? There is something so tender, so innocent, so trusting about two souls uniting *pour le meilleur et pour le pire, jusqu'à ce que la mort nous sépare!*

Next, we raced back to our *résidence hôtelière* to put sheets on our bed (Jean-Marc located a janitor who tossed him a duffel bag of bleached linens) and change for the dressy evening reception. Everything had gone incredibly smoothly up till now, so when I saw my horrible, chipped toenail polish, *pas de panique!* I simply let it go. (I would not trade all that walking and sightseeing around the island for a perfect manicure!)

Back at the reception in a picturesque *hameau*, we joined the bride, groom, and over a hundred *invités* for a night of dining, dancing, and toasting to *une vie à deux*. I missed my chance to offer any guidance to the young couple, but now, in retrospect, I suppose one piece of advice I could give would be to incorporate this golden phrase, adopted on this romantic getaway: *"Je te suis!"* I will follow you! (And then to take turns saying it to each other throughout your marriage.)

Back on the airplane, buckled in and heading home, I am amazed at how smoothly our four-day race to Brittany went. Like the shores of *Bréhat*, where the tide comes in and goes out, so do our fears, doubts, needs, wants, and moods. We just have to keep our eyes on the horizon, remembering that every little thing will work itself out. As I sit next to Jean-Marc, I reflect on how this trip, with its minor challenges and beautiful moments, has reinforced our bond. "*Je te suis, chéri,*" I whisper, knowing that these words mean more than just a willingness to follow. They represent trust, love, and a lifelong partnership. No matter where life takes us, I pray we will navigate it together, sometimes leading, sometimes following, but always side by side.

FRENCH VOCABULARY

le mariage
a wedding

le fiancé (la fiancée)
betrothed

le périple
journey

la robe
dress

la jupe
skirt

la chemise
shirt

la vedette
the ferry

pédaler
to pedal

ouf!
whew!

l'embarcadère (m)
the dock

le séjour
stay

'apéro (m)
pre-dinner drink/snack

le pain au chocolat
chocolate croissant

le café crème
coffee with milk

le phare du Paon
the Paon lighthouse

Je te suis
I will follow you

L'hortensia (m)
hydrangea

la marche
a walk

la confiture
jam

le petit marché
the little market

**Servez-vous
et laissez les sous
dans la caisse
s'il vous plaît**
Serve yourself and
leave the money in
the cash box

le pin parasol
umbrella pine

le tamaris
tamarisk
(a shrub with
feathery leaves
and pink or
white flowers)

l'huître (f)
oyster

**la brandade
de morue**
cod brandade
(a dish made
with salted cod
and potatoes)

l'île (f)
island

de rigueur
required
or essential

le croissant
a French
crescent-shaped roll
made of sweet flaky
pastry, often eaten
for breakfast.

l'église
church

**pour le meilleur
et pour le pire,
jusqu'à ce que la
mort nous sépare**
for better or for
worse, until death
do us part

**une résidence
hôtelière**
a hotel residence

pas de panique
no worries

un hameau
a hamlet

un(e) invité(e)
a guest

une vie à deux
a life together

**mon chéri
(ma chérie)**
my dear,
my darling

26

UN AUXILIAIRE DE VIE

When I stop to think about it, July has been the most challenging month of this year so far. Though it began with excellent news (Mom's insurance came through!) and the joy of our 30th wedding anniversary celebration for Jean-Marc and me, tensions were rising between mother and daughter here at our multi-generational home. It seemed the honeymoon phase of this caregiving journey we are on together was over. Nurse Kristi was all but fired! Then the heatwave hit, followed by a strange plague of mites (and their bites), making it feel like I had arrived at the gates of hell.

For some reason, those venom-filled *acariens* (possibly "*les pyémotes*"—our friend Pierre suggested) were attacking me with a vengeance! These pests, which come out in spring and summer, nest inside wood, infesting places like the fireplace, antique furniture, and perhaps even the wooden knobs where I hang my bathrobe. Whereas six weeks ago I received a dozen or so of these bites, this time there were too many to count. The venomous *piqûres* turned into itchy welts, and I was absolutely miserable by Thursday when we were set to go to *un vernissage* at Château La Tour de l'Evêque, where our son, Max, is in charge of wine export.

Waking up Friday morning, itching and unable to scratch, I was desperate. *"Je vais pleurer!"* I said to Jean-Marc. I'm learning it helps to say the words "I am going to cry" or "I feel like crying" when my body can't release tears of despair or frustration. For one, it allows my husband to know I'm at a very low point. Ironically, a 30-second emotional commercial on TV, a wedding, or a baptism can make me bawl instantly. But other matters of the heart and, in this case, psyche, remain invisible when I shut down.

Just when it seemed I could take the torture no longer, my daughter came into the room. "How are you doing, Mom?"

After I let it all out—the unbearable bites and the wicked heat—Jackie assured me: *"Ça passera."* My daughter had unknowingly cited one of my favorite assurances, *This too shall pass*, and the effect was immediate. The itching subsided in light of the thought that this situation would not last forever. Jackie was right. This current trial would soon be over, and things would patch up between Mom and me—just give it time.

In the days following the emotional and physical release, a series of serendipitous encounters took place as friends and helpers came out of the woodwork (instead of those pesky mites!). It began when I was walking back from the pharmacy and a woman on the opposite *trottoir* said hello. I recognized her because of her chocolate labrador. *"Comment allez-vous?"* she said, reaching out.

"Très bien, merci!" I was giddy, suddenly imagining an invitation to her *avant-garde* bungalow, which I'd witnessed being renovated all last year!

A few blocks later, I recognized another local and her pit bull. We've run into each other a few times at the farmers market and at *les roches plates*, the flat rocks where we swim. *"Coucou!"* she said, crossing the street. We chatted on the sidewalk like old friends. Counting my blessings on the way home, I now had the energy to call on another neighbor I'd met at the beach a year ago while she was training her Australian Shepherd. Nathalie, it turns out, is a nurse. When I explained to her that my mom needed a weekly injection and twice-weekly blood samples, as prescribed recently by her doctor, Nathalie said she could help, and true to her word, she's been here almost every day this week. And in her absence, she's sent Nicolas, who Mom also likes a lot!

Then, Sunday, while walking to church, I stopped to look at a rack of sundresses (desperate for something cool to wear in this *canicule*) when a young lady inside the store came out. "Kristi?"

"Yes…"

"It's Fiona! We met at the clothing store where I used to work."

"Yes, yes! I remember you." How could I forget this friendly, helpful and professional woman who was about my daughter's age? She made an impression on me last fall when I was preparing for a trip to Paris. *"Comment ça va?"* I smiled.

"Sadly, I was laid off! Thankfully, I found temporary work."

"I'm so sorry you lost your job. What would you like to do?"

"I'd like to be an *auxiliaire de vie* and help seniors."

What a coincidence! "Just this week," I explained, "I received a flyer in the mail for a local service offering in-home assistance. I saved it as I am looking for someone to assist my mom! Maybe we can work something out?"

With promises to keep in touch we hugged, and I continued on my way to church, feeling so blessed I couldn't imagine *le prédicateur* could top this with a more hopeful message. But he did, and it was, in a nutshell, about opening our hearts: "Jesus stands at the door knocking, but the doorknob is on our side of the door," said the Irish preacher, in perfect French, at our tiny local *église baptiste*.

Well, this week, dear reader, I opened the door, *and look at all the angels who rushed in!*

It is hard to ask for help, but once you do, things have a way of falling into place. Now that Nathalie and Nicolas are here and Fiona is on the way, it is having an effect on both Mom and me. We're both up early and dressed, dusting off our counters and

preparing for these angels to help a couple of would-be hermits. While I still have some doubts as to whether I can keep up with the regular visitors, I understand that change is good and will keep us from falling into a pit.

Speaking of pits and hell, my mite bites are fading, and I am cooling down with the help of regular splashes of water from the sink, a few ceiling fans, and some sundresses I've located in my bags of summer clothes that I need to sort out. Maybe Fiona can help me too?

I'll wrap up this entry with a giant hug to all of you. It's surprising how much love manifests when we finally reach for that doorknob. Remember, it's on the inside of *la porte*! Only you can reach it. Love is on the outside knocking.

POST NOTES: The next morning, I hurried over to Mom's to wake her before Nurse Nathalie arrived. I was greeted with the biggest hug and several "I LOVE YOUs."

"You know you are my favorite person," I assured Mom, hugging her back. Next time Mom is at a low point, as I was recently, I'm going to share my tip: just say the words "*J'ai besoin de pleurer*"— I need to cry. You may or may not experience a cathartic release, but you'll have gotten the words out.

FRENCH VOCABULARY

un(e) auxiliaire de vie
caregiver

l'acariens (m)
mite

le pyémote (m)
pyemote
(a type of mite)

la piqûre
bite, sting

le vernissage
private viewing

Je vais pleurer
I am going to cry

ça passera
this will be over
(soon)

le trottoir
the sidewalk

Comment allez-vous?
How are you?

Très bien, merci!
Very well,
thank you!

avant-garde
cutting-edge

les roches plates (f)
the flat rocks

Coucou
Hi

la canicule
heatwave

Comment ça va?
How are you?

le prédicateur
preacher

l'église baptiste (f)
Baptist church

la porte
the door

J'ai besoin de pleurer
I need to cry

AUGUST
Août

27

L'EMBARRAS DU CHOIX

When I asked readers to help choose a cover design for my book, the response was *spectaculaire*. Thank you for scrutinizing all eight *couverture*s, for voting, and for commenting on the title and graphics. I learned so much from your feedback, and now I'm as confused as ever.

Just kidding. *Je rigole!* I can handle it. *Je gère!*

One thing I wasn't managing so well is people. You see, I also asked for volunteers to proofread my work, and the response knocked my socks off. It was, as the French say, *l'embarras du choix*: a situation where so many good options make it difficult, if not impossible, to choose. And when these options are people—instead of, say, so many *parfums* at the ice cream stand—it's hard to pick just one.

As I lay beneath our noisy ceiling fan, sweating and fretting about my book and beyond ("beyond" meaning my home and family, my dog, this current heatwave, and *le ménage*) I felt *dépassée* by it all. With my son renting out his apartment on Airbnb and moving back home with his *petite amie*, we have a full house this first week of August. The downstairs bathroom is flooded with towels, four of us have colds, and this place feels like *Animal House*!

Meanwhile, over at Book Project Central (the little workstation I set up in our cramped *cafoutche*, amidst the suitcases, the ironing board, and the vacuum), my phone began pinging nonstop as my Book Cover Poll on Facebook and Instagram delivered results in real time. The social media feedback was manageable (I could "heart" every response to express thanks), but my inbox was expanding before my very eyes. How to kindly acknowledge all these emailed responses? There was simply no way to keep up! Why not throw in the towel now? Speaking of which…

When my phone pinged one more time, I opened Messenger to experience a much-needed chuckle. A picture of a now-orderly towel rack with a digitalized name tag over each *serviette*! *Génial! Merci*, Max, for civilizing the towel situation! After washing and line-drying our towels, my son defrosted our icy freezer, emptied the vacuum cleaner, and scrubbed the filter before asking, "What

A Year in a French Life 2024 by Kristin Espinasse • Cover designs by TLC Book Design • July 24, 2024

else can I do for you?" And just like that, help, like the cold virus we all caught, was now spreading rapidly! Jean-Marc took Grandma to the grocery store, Jackie brought two big salads home for dinner, Ana set the table, Grandma Jules was in charge of watering the garden, Ricci and Izzy were keeping the floors licked clean, and so on and so forth *et cetera pantoufle*!

(Have I told you about my favorite, totally obsolete and nonsensical French expression, *et cetera pantoufle*—"and so on slipper"? Finally, the chance to use it here!)

Meanwhile, I began to answer emails when a new stream of feedback flooded my phone screen: readers were pointing out *un petit souci* with the title of my memoir, which included the year these essays were written. "Don't put 2024. This would date the book!" Whoops! I'd forgotten to mention this is a book series. I am gathering each year's stories into a collection under the umbrella title *"A Year in a French Life."* This first book would be *"A Year in a French Life: 2024."* The next would be *"A Year in a French Life: 2025,"* *et cetera pantoufle…*

But I now see your point. Including the date might deter potential readers. One solution would be to use one of the chapter titles as the subtitle. For example: *"A Year in a French Life: L'Embarras du Choix."* Can you picture this now? While "spoiled for choice" doesn't exactly summarize the 2024 stories, it is a catchy way to distinguish between the editions, *n'est-ce pas?* Another chapter in this book is *"Il devait en être ainsi"* (or "Predestined"…tell me if that doesn't sound intriguing!). Other chapters/potential subtitles include:

- *"Le Bonheur"* ("Happiness")
- *"Bien Joué"* ("Well Done!")

- "*Jamais Deux Sans Trois*" ("Good things come in Threes." However, it can also mean "Bad Things Come in Threes." This title might not be good for marketing…)

Even with some of the pieces of this project coming together, I tossed and turned all weekend despite trying to focus on the Olympics. During judo, *l'escrime*, and pole-vaulting, my mind chattered on and on: *I must answer all these emails! I've got to send off my manuscript…but to whom?* Suddenly, all these potential volunteers posed a logistical conundrum: how would each reader record their edits? (In Microsoft Word there is some sort of "live" option, where editors can go right into the document and correct or change text. But isn't that risky? And what would it be like to receive an influx of live edits from dozens of readers? I could just see my manuscript pole-vaulting all over the place with each added edit!)

As I agonized over how to orchestrate this book project, the word surrender swooped in, once again, to offer relief. Surrender…a theme visited every so often in this journal: literally *se rendre*. It means to be still and let the doubts, fears, and unknowns wash right over, like a cool stream of melted ice cream during a heatwave. Surrendering takes faith and practice—a lot of both—but it is as vital as ice cream (according to Grandma Jules, who brought back a little too much of it from the grocery store…). We must trust that when we let go everything will eventually come together, things will get done, and we will show up on time. By surrendering here and now we allow the help at hand—whether divine or, like my readers, sublime—to manifest. Finally, we have stepped out of the way, to find ourselves in the midst of grace.

FRENCH VOCABULARY

l'embarras du choix
too many good options

spectaculaire
spectacular

la couverture (du livre)
(book) covers

je rigole
just kidding

je gère
I can handle it

le parfum
flavor

le ménage
household chores

dépassé(e)
overwhelmed

la petite amie
girlfriend

le cafoutche
storage room
(a Marseille term)

la serviette
towel

génial(e)
brilliant

merci
thank you

et cetera pantoufle
and so on
and so forth

un petit souci
a little issue

n'est-ce pas
isn't it

Il devait en être ainsi
meant to be
(predestined)

le bonheur
happiness

bien joué
well done

jamais deux sans trois
good (or bad) things
come in threes

l'escrime
fencing

se rendre
to surrender

28

À FLEUR DE PEAU

woke up this morning with a tinge of the blues. In French, they call it *le cafard*, a condition I'm not too familiar with—anxiety being my usual companion—*mais ça arrive*. The elusive feeling came on suddenly and, like a drop of dye in a glass of water, it is slowly spreading, clouding my environment.

I have not read Charles Baudelaire's *Les Fleurs du Mal* but it introduced the concept of *le cafard*, or those dark thoughts that can invade the mind, much like how cockroaches infest a house. Those repugnant beetles are ugly, icky, and even a bit sticky, which is how heavy feelings are, too. *J'ai le cafard* literally means *I have the cockroach*.

Have you noticed how *la déprime* is tangible? The blues share something in common with *un bleu* (a bruise); both are physical. They reside just beneath or on the surface of the skin, *à fleur de peau* (what a lovely expression, but that is as poetic and as French as depression gets. *Le cafard* is latent, articulated only in retrospect).

As much as we wish this clingy sentiment would flee, it may be there to teach you and me. *Quelle est la leçon?* Could it be about

understanding others with depression, recognizing when to slow down, or acknowledging the need for connection? Perhaps this lull I feel after last week's full house—Max and Ana are back at the apartment, and Jean-Marc is away—helps me realize that I may not enjoy being alone as much as I thought.

Allez, Ricci! On y va! My dog and I go for a walk to try to shake things off, but it only makes me aware of my thoughts: *Dois-je prendre des antidépresseurs? Would medication make me lazy or unproductive? Could that be a good thing? No!* I realize I feel better when I'm engaged in work. Don't we all? Just last night, my daughter expressed doubts about her upcoming two-week break before she begins her master's program. She knows herself well and finds that she's happiest—or at least less depressed—when busy.

It all seems to boil down to staying occupied, or, rather, *staying engaged.* Even the folks in Paris struggle with *Métro-Boulot-Dodo*—or the monotonous cycle of "commute-work-sleep"—another form of depression born from repetitive routine. While my own die-hard routine may be contributing to these low-grade feelings, working through this story today has kept me engaged and, as we near the end, it feels like an achievement. Finishing something, whether a morning walk or a letter to a friend, brings a sense of relief. It may be a fleeting high, but right now, I'm happy to report, there's not a *cafard* in sight!

FRENCH VOCABULARY

à fleur de peau
under/on the
surface of the skin

le cafard
blues

mais ça arrive
but it happens

Les Fleurs du Mal
The Flowers of Evil

J'ai le cafard
I've got the blues

la déprime
depression

un bleu
a bruise

**Quelle est
la leçon?**
What is the lesson?

**Allez, Ricci!
On y va!**
Come on, Ricci!
Let's go!

**Dois-je
prendre des
antidépresseurs?**
Should I take
antidepressants?

**Métro-Boulot-
Dodo**
the daily grind

29
ÉPANOUISSEMENT

*R*icci is about to turn four, and it is remarkable how much she has enriched our lives since she bounded into our home from a remote barn in central France. What began as a leap of faith has evolved into a profound *complicité*—one that makes me confront an unexpected dilemma: the deep, sometimes surprising love I feel for Ricci compared to the affection I had for our previous dogs. It feels almost taboo to even talk about *un chien favori* when you've had two lovely dogs before her. As I process these feelings, I wanted to take a moment to honor our *rescapée* on this, the week of her birthday.

I still can't believe how lucky we are to have this beautiful, funny, stubborn, and adorably clumsy American Shepherd as our new family dog. Jean-Marc and I regularly remark: "It's a good thing *I* found her!" While we enjoy teasing each other, the uncomfortable truth is that Ricci's fate was decided by a flip of the coin. Heads, we bring home this unknown, possibly problematic dog. Tails, we leave her…to her fate. I couldn't bear the thought of that. *The decision was quickly made!*

To think I ever had doubts about how it would all work out the day we collected Ricci from a dog, cow, and cannabis farm in Auvergne. The owner was phasing out the puppy side of her business, and that's how we ended up bringing home this blue-eyed mama. Strangely, she did not resist as we carried her away without a leash, a collar, or even the slightest idea of who we were and where she was going. Throughout the five-hour ride home she was silent, barely moving from my lap, which soon became a pool of drool from her unspoken stress.

She perked up upon arrival! In those early days, our adoptee was so unpredictable: she tried to escape, trembled for weeks, growled at other dogs, nipped at family members, and peed all over our home. To top it off, she had the most offensive breath—*haleine* so bad it rivaled *les Époisses de Bourgogne*, one of the stinkiest cheeses in France.

Then there was her *prénom*, which was difficult for me to pronounce (I've never been good at rolling those French "r"s. I thought to change her name, but given how disoriented she was, it didn't seem like a good idea).

Despite the negatives, we saw Ricci ("*RRREE-CHEE*") for what she was, a displaced dog who, once we earned her trust, would get better. Around that time a reader named Lin shared the "3:3:3 Rule" for rescue dogs: in three days, she would become familiar with her new surroundings, in three weeks she'd be comfortable with her environment, and in three months she'd feel secure and set in her routine. I hung on to this promise as our newest family member progressed through the various *étapes*. With every day that passed, we watched Ricci slowly blossom from a skittish, uncertain dog into a confident, affectionate companion. The first time her little nub of a tail wagged (you had to look closely because her *queue* had been docked), the moment she finally slept through the night, the day she jumped into my lap—each of these was a sign

that the 3:3:3 Rule was working. It was a gradual transformation, but each step was a victory, for Ricci and for us.

Just when things were coming together, there was a crisis. Ricci panicked after a sudden *bruit* at the farmers market and ran off. During the chase, with Ricci fleeing beside traffic, our short life together flashed before my eyes: all the progress she'd made, all the trust we'd built…only for her to be running away when she needed me most!

When finally she landed in my arms, saved by the quick action of a few locals, I wasn't about to let her go again. It took weeks before I began to trust her. I learned our little Houdini could wiggle right out of her harness as she did when Jean-Marc brought her to the dock to wait for him while he worked on his boat.

Eventually, we felt confident enough to give her some slack while strolling along the boardwalk. She's gradually adapting to *le grincement* of delivery truck doors, the pop! of a deflating paddle board, and the whir and grumble of the big, bad streetcleaner truck.

These days she leaps with joy onto our couch (sometimes slamming into the side of it, completely unharmed, if aerodynamically challenged...) where she eventually settles in the curve of my legs to fall asleep. I love her so much I could burst. "Mom," I say, seated next to Jules, Ricci cuddled in between us, "I...I think she is my favorite dog." I could only admit this to my own Mom, as saying it to anyone else seems taboo. It would be as shocking as choosing a favorite kid.

We sit in silence, stroking Ricci, remembering our beloved golden retriever, who passed away two summers ago. "I think Smokey picked Ricci out for us," I whisper. The idea is comforting and takes away some of the guilt I feel for loving Ricci so much. Suddenly, I am reminded of the day I realized I loved Smokey more than our first dog, Breizh...I remember feeling bad about that, too!

I've come to realize that with each new dog, my heart has grown bigger, not because one dog is better than the other, but because each has taught me to love more deeply. As someone once said: *Un nouveau chien ne remplace jamais un vieux chien, il ne fait qu'agrandir le cœur.* A new dog never replaces an old dog, it only enlarges the heart.

Seeing Ricci's (and our own) *épanouissement* over the past year has only reinforced this truth. No wonder my heart is bursting with love. *Joyeux Anniversaire, Ricci, et merci!*

FRENCH VOCABULARY

l'épanouissement (m)
the blossoming/ flourishing

la complicité
the bond/ connection

le chien favori
favorite dog

un(e) rescap(é)e
a rescue dog

l'haleine (f)
the breath

les Époisses de Bourgogne
Époisses cheese from Burgundy

le prénom
first name

les étapes (f)
the stages

la queue
the tail

le bruit
noise

le grincement
the creaking

Un nouveau chien ne remplace jamais un vieux chien, il ne fait qu'agrandir le cœur
A new dog never replaces an old dog, it only enlarges the heart

Joyeux Anniversaire, Ricci, et merci!
Happy Birthday, Ricci, and thank you!

30
REPOSE
EN PAIX

*J*t is just after 6 a.m., and my husband is on his way out to harvest at a friend's vineyard in Bandol. Ever since we sold our last *domaine*, Jean-Marc has managed to keep his feet consistently in (or near) a bucket of grapes. I'm happy for him, and seeing the smile on his face as he kisses me goodbye reminds me to always encourage him to follow his path.

As Chief Grape left the room, I felt an inkling to pray for him. Though it's been years since he struggled with *le cafard*, our emotional needs and spiritual growth don't suddenly end when we feel better. Positive thoughts and prayers are strengtheners, and faith and hope are what keep us going. My wish for each family member is always the same: that they will grow closer to *leur source de vie*.

I hear the jingle bell on the front door signaling someone's left the house. "Lord, as Jean-Marc goes out into the vineyard today, his sacred place, please speak to his heart." I didn't have further instructions for God, only one additional request: "Could you also please show me a sign? I know we are not supposed to ask for signs, but anything at all, God, to let me know you are working in his heart."

With that, my day began. I wrangled with family members, trying to get everyone—from my dog to Grandma—settled so I could eventually find some peace and quiet to meet my deadlines. Besides these weekly blog posts, I have a bi-monthly column due soon for *France Today* and a book project I'm struggling to keep up with.

First order of the day: get my stubborn dog out for a walk. With Ricci straining against the leash, I reached down and scooped her up. "There! *ON VA MARCHER!*" After fits and starts around the neighborhood, we made it home in time to quickly scramble a few eggs (I hear protein is a good mood stabilizer. Hopefully it helps with female hormones too—mine, this time, and not Ricci's…).

I now needed to get Mom sorted out—not that Jules felt the same need. But she couldn't deny she needed groceries, and it was time to help change her sheets. Only, after Mom's new helper, Fiona, returned from the store, Mom threw a wrench in my plans by deciding the bed linen change would have to wait. What's more, she sent Fiona back to my place to change *my* sheets. (It turns out this was all a lack of communication, which happens often in a bilingual household!)

Tensions were growing, lunch preparation loomed in the air, and I tried to focus on my writing, as story ideas superimposed one over the other, adding to the confusion. Just when I settled down to sort things out, Jackie asked if I could hang out her laundry as she was running late for work. Then Max telephoned for a favor: would I follow him to the repair shop to drop off his company car? And just like that, *rebelote!*—we were back on the jungle train again!

Somehow, we monkeys managed to get through the day: Jean-Marc processed more grapes, Mom got clean sheets, Jackie made it to work on time, Max's car was fixed, and I wrote a workable draft for this blog. As usual, the pressure began to ease when I checked in to say goodnight to Mom and found her in a happy mood (watching horse videos on YouTube does that). "Kristi! You'll never believe what happened!" she said. "Earlier, I was lying here in bed, wishing for something sweet to eat after dinner. A moment later, Jean-Marc came in with two ice cream bars! Isn't that incredible?"

Incredible? Yes, on so many levels. Suddenly, I remembered the prayer I had said earlier and hurried home to tell Jean-Marc about *le signe de là-haut*. He smiled, more in amusement than conviction, but that was good enough for me. As I once read, "*Le sourire est chez l'homme l'empreinte de Dieu*"—the smile is in man the imprint of God.*

But, dear reader, our story doesn't end here, nor do God's mysterious ways. When evening came, I asked Jean-Marc if he happened to have a photo of the vineyard where he was harvesting that morning—something to illustrate the blog post I was working on.

"The only photo I have is with Lou Bogue."

"Lou Bogue?"

"Yes, Lou harvested with me at that same vineyard several years ago."

That's when I recalled a visit from one of my readers, Lou. At the age of 83, with shoulder-length silver locks and a boyish grin, he helped us harvest at our first vineyard, Domaine Rouge-Bleu. When we moved to La Ciotat, he traveled to visit us. By then, he was in his early 90s. I'll never forget taking Lou to lunch and leaving him to explore *le centre-ville* that afternoon. He insisted he'd find his way back to his Airbnb, but by early evening, Jean-Marc had an inkling of his own and felt a strong urge to get in his car and go searching for Lou…

Lo and behold, there at the old port, Lou was standing on a corner, waiting for a bus back to his rental. Only there were no more buses that evening. Just when a stranger wandered up to Lou, soliciting for something, Jean-Marc quickly pulled up to the curb.

He reached over to open the passenger door and Lou, ever chipper (and a little *pompette* after leaving one of the local bars…), thanked him for the ride home. Lou eventually returned to Florida and kept in touch with me via Facebook, as he had for years. In fact, he was one of my first blog readers! As always, he said he was planning a trip to see us. He was 95 the last time he made this promise.

After Jean-Marc reminded me of the harvest with Lou, I went over to Facebook to contact him for permission to post his photo. Only, instead of his usual update, there was a message from his daughter:

"…We want to thank all who've shared cards and their prayers after the recent loss of my dad, Louis Bogue, in Dunedin, Florida. He lived a full 96 years and passed in peaceful sleep after being surrounded by family on February 15, 2024. We will celebrate his life on Father's Day in Atlanta with a book we are creating of his golf journey and adventure-filled life. We invite you to share sentiments and photos…"

I am so sad to learn Lou is no longer among us, and upset I missed the chance to say goodbye. It all brings me back to my driven nature, as I crack the whip at the beginning of another day. Why do I always feel so rushed to get everything done "on time"? Just what is "on time" when you are on a schedule of your own making?

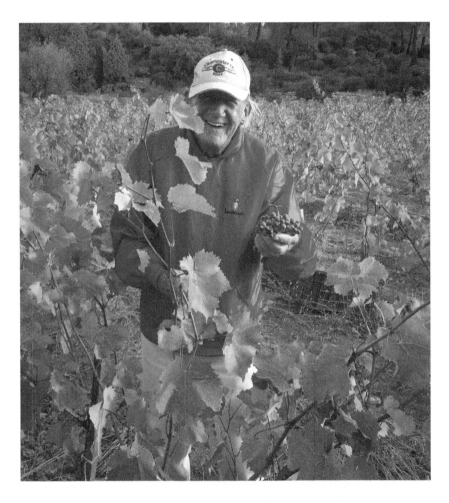

I ask myself, finally, "Whether I get the sheets changed today or whether I'm late saying *adieu* to a dearly departed friend —*what is time in the face of eternity?*"

I can almost hear Lou's voice, his wisdom echoing back an answer: "Time, *mon amie*, is eternal when you do everything with love. So sit back, smile, and remember your husband, your family, and your friends. Have a little more fun in life. Get out there and enjoy some adventures. Love life!"

Thank you, Lou, for keeping in touch and for always promising to get back to France. I love you! I did not tell you directly or often enough how much you impressed me with your plans. If I'm honest, this middle-aged mess was a little suspicious of your endless youth—and now regrets not asking you your secret (which may have been shared in the paragraph above)! In your mid-90s, your excitement and verve for life, for friends, and your love for France were stronger than ever. You wore a permanent smile, *l'empreinte de Dieu*. Sign of signs!

I like a story to come full circle, so let's return to that glorious *vignoble* in Bandol, where my husband was just beginning the harvest. In that paradisical setting, I prayed that God would work in his heart and send me some kind of message. I know we're not supposed to ask for signs from God—perhaps that's why I received one from an old friend instead. *Repose en paix*, Lou. In memory of you, I'm going to try to slow down, chill out, and follow in your loving footsteps.

After typing the last line of this story, I stumbled upon an old email reply from Lou:

"Yes, a young girl's dreams of finding a way of life that will bring all those dreams to fruition is a hard journey. Sometimes it's long and tedious, and sometimes a move to a completely new environment opens the door to understanding what you really want out of life. As the saying goes, NOTHING VEN-TURED—NOTHING GAINED. Another big secret of life: KEEP MOVING forward, never backward."

* The smile quote is by Robert Choin

FRENCH VOCABULARY

repose en paix
rest in peace

le domaine
the estate, vineyard

le cafard

leur source (f)
their source

de vie
of life

on va marcher
we are going to walk

rebelote
here we go again

le signe de là-haut
the sign from above

le sourire est chez l'homme l'empreinte de Dieu
the smile is in man the imprint of God

le centre-ville
the town center

pompette
tipsy

adieu
goodbye forever

mon ami(e)
my friend

l'empreinte de Dieu
the imprint of God

le vignoble
vineyard

SEPTEMBER
Septembre

SEPTEMBER

31

À TABLE!

*E*ver since we lost our picnic table in a fire last year, we've struggled to find a suitable replacement. With no place to gather for outdoor meals, we resorted to lugging our dining table outside that first summer, enjoying lunch or dinner under the open sky whenever the weather was good. We managed this way until Christmas when eleven of us gathered around for *le repas de Noël*. In the new year, when it became too cold *pour dîner dehors*, we carried our dining table back into the house, where it belonged.

Come springtime, we rustled up a round metal table from our garden, in time to enjoy meals out on *la terrasse* again. Finally, by summer's end, Jean-Marc saw an ad in Facebook Marketplace—and there she was, a wooden beauty that would become our new centerpiece for *l'heure de l'apéro*, lunch, dinner, or even work.

As fast as you can say à table my husband bought it. "Our jeep isn't big enough to transport it," Jean-Marc explained, on returning from the seller's house. "But the man said he would be able to help."

Ricci and I were heading to Mom's around the side of our house when the table arrived. Jean-Marc had invited the seller to sit down for an ice-cold *mousse* after he had generously assisted with the delivery. (He had a more spacious *fourgonnette*.) Beyond just transporting the table, the man had taken the time to treat the wood with *l'huile de lin*—a courtesy that didn't go unnoticed.

The older man was somewhat winded as he took a seat at his former table, his salt-and-pepper locks damp from the oppressive heatwave. He wore a classic white *marcel* and a pair of shorts. "*Bonjour, Monsieur!*" I said, breezing by. "*Oh, qu'elle est belle cette table. Merci!*" After a hasty hello, I disappeared to Mom's for some trivial matter, leaving the men to finish up business. I made it as far as the driveway when a gnawing feeling inside made me realize I'd ignored our visitor. I brushed it aside, reminding myself he was but a stranger.

Before long, we were enjoying meals around our second-hand table. *Nickel!* Max said, admiring its oval design, which rounded out the seating to 8. "We could even squeeze in two more," Jackie noted. Everyone was enthusiastic, but none more than Jules, who spontaneously slipped her son-in-law 200 euros to pay for it. "It's beautiful! I love it!" she said. Jean-Marc had truly outdone himself, finding the perfect table for just 180 euros—and with 5 chairs included, *à ce prix-là, c'était une aubaine!* (And with the extra cash he could buy Grandma some more ice cream to thank her for picking up the tab!)

One morning while we were having our coffee, I asked Jean-Marc about the table's history. "Why was the man selling it?"

"Oh," Jean-Marc sighed. "He was being evicted from the property, where he was renting a little *cabanon.*"

"Evicted. That's terrible!"

Jean-Marc explained that the man had a home in Marseille, but this modest cabin had been his *pied-à-terre* for thirty-five years. Like many *Marseillais* back in the day, he would escape the city for "*la campagne,*" sharing this seaside terrain with a few other families, each with their own *petite cabane* on the property.

Now those buildings will be demolished, with little regard for the people who once made memories there. All to make room for yet another *programme immobilier*—brand new condos. With the growth and rising popularity of our town—a former industrial shipping hub now catering to yachts—the demographics are shifting, and the demand for real estate is soaring.

Sadly, this longtime resident must leave. With the help of his daughter, the elderly man listed his few possessions and packed up his modest abode to return to the outskirts of Marseille.

As Jean-Marc told the story, I pictured the man at this very table, where he and others had once gathered after returning from *la pêche* or a hike in the fragrant hills above La Ciotat. They might have enjoyed a round of *pastis* followed by a homemade *soupe de poisson*. A doze under the shady parasol pine completed the perfect *journée*.

Those halcyon days were fading, and soon the pine tree would be gone too. When Monsieur sat at the table for the last time, sharing a refreshment with Jean-Marc, a chapter of his life was coming to a poignant close…

…Yet, a new chapter for the table was just beginning, with the man forever intertwined in its story. His soul—and even his sweat—became part of it over the years, and again at the farewell delivery, as salty droplets mingled with the condensation from the men's cool beers, anointing the wood below…

We will all enjoy this table, even more than the one we have lost. Though I missed the chance to connect with a venerable character, my hasty hello now serves as a reminder to focus on what matters most in life: the people we meet and their stories. As the saying goes:

Ne négligez pas de pratiquer l'hospitalité. Car certains, en l'exerçant, ont accueilli des anges sans le savoir.

Do not forget to show hospitality to strangers, for by so doing some people have shown hospitality to angels without knowing it.

FRENCH VOCABULARY

à table!
to the table!

le repas de Noël
Christmas meal

pour dîner dehors
to dine outside

la terrasse
patio, terrace

l'heure de l'apéro (f)
aperitif hour

la mousse
beer (informally)

la fourgonnette
the van

l'huile de lin (f)
linseed oil

le marcel
tank top

**Bonjour,
Monsieur!**
Hello, sir!

**Oh, qu'elle est belle
cette table. Merci!**
Oh, how beautiful
this table is.
Thank you!

Nickel!
Perfect!

**à ce prix-là, c'était
une aubaine!**
at that price,
it was a bargain!

le cabanon
the cabin

le pied-à-terre
second home

**Marseillais,
Marseillaise**
someone from
Marseille

la campagne
the countryside

la petite cabane
the little hut

**le programme
immobilier**
real estate
development

la pêche
fishing

le pastis
anise-flavored spirit

**la soupe
de poisson**
fish soup

la journée
the day

**Ne négligez pas
de pratiquer
l'hospitalité.
Car certains,
en l'exerçant, ont
accueilli des anges
sans le savoir.**
Do not forget
to show hospitality
to strangers,
for by so doing some
people have shown
hospitality to angels
without knowing it.

(Hebrews 13:2)

32
UNE NUIT BLANCHE

The first week of fall had me tossing and turning like a leaf spiraling from a tree. It began Saturday night when I woke with a start. But it wasn't *un cauchemar* that jolted me awake. No, it was my husband's phone. Specifically—it was that annoying PING! of instant messaging.

I felt a low, deep groan rising from somewhere in my being. *Pouah!* he forgot to turn off his phone—again! Resisting the urge to react further, I lay there quietly in the dark as Jean-Marc fumbled for his *téléphone portable*, putting it on airplane mode.

Ouaf! Ouaf! Ouaf! Now our dog was awake and excited at the chance to go outside after midnight.

"*Dodo, Ricci! Dodo!*" Jean-Marc ordered our little shepherd to go back to sleep, as if it were that easy. Well, apparently it was for the man who'd woken us all up!

Within minutes, Jean-Marc's steady breathing told me he was fast asleep again. Meanwhile, I was wide awake—and more than a little annoyed to have been pulled from such a satisfying *sommeil*.

Even if I decided right away to let this little resentment go, and get on with the business of trying to fall back to sleep, the universe seemed to have other plans…such as resolving a long-standing cultural divide. You see, there was a time—before coming to France—when I would have rallied in the face of challenges. But after 30 years in the *Hexagone*, I grumble—*je râle*—at the slightest inconvenience! Along with winning the Olympic gold in complaining, the French are seasoned doubters. Their *tout est impossible* attitude stands in stark contrast to my "where there's a will, there's a way" American upbringing.

Lying there, eyes wide open, I began to wonder if anything was possible tonight. Could I manage to fall back asleep? My mind quickly shifted, though, as another thought took over: What time is it? I resisted the urge to check the clock, knowing it would only make things worse…

I started wondering if Jackie had made it home safely. She'd left for Cassis in the late afternoon to pick up her final paycheck at the hotel. "I'm meeting a friend for a drink after," she said, before driving off. It was so quiet outside that the eerie call of the owl echoed through the streets of our neighborhood. It must be past three… Suddenly, all I could think of was the dark, winding road between Cassis and home. Tossing and turning, I debated getting up to check if my daughter's car was in the driveway. But if it wasn't…I'd go into full panic mode. So I lay there frozen.

Grrh! She could have texted me! I grumbled (not that I would've heard the ping on MY phone, which was in airplane mode). After 30 minutes of inner back-and-forth, I finally reached for my phone to check the time. 3:30 a.m.! *Mais où-est-elle?!* A quick call revealed she was fine—enjoying the lively port of Cassis, one last summer night with friends.

Bon, I thought, now I'll be able to sleep. But just as I patted my pillow and settled in, I remembered Mom's upcoming doctors' appointments in Marseille. The thought of driving to the city, dealing with the hospital, and then driving back after dark began to weigh on me as I have difficulty seeing beyond the windshield at night. Why is that doctor always *en retard?* If she weren't so very late each time, I wouldn't have to worry about driving after sundown! Worse than complaining I was now blaming. This was no way to begin to find peace in the middle of the night—or anywhere in life!

Still wide awake, I decided to rally…instead of *râler*, or complain. If I was going to lie there and think a lot, I'd think pleasant thoughts! I remembered an amusing phone call I'd had earlier with my son. Max was driving with his girlfriend when he rang me here at home:

"Hey Mom, I'll pick you up at 11 tomorrow for Pilates," he said. Max had a guest pass and invited me to join him at his gym in Saint Cyr-sur-Mer, but I was skeptical.

"Will I need to fill out any forms? What do I bring? How long is the class?" I asked, picturing a room full of perfect Pilates people.

"You'll just need a towel and a bottle of water."

"That's it? There won't be any papers to fill out—some kind of satisfaction survey?"

"No, Mom. But you will go through security."

At that, I imagined a TSA-style line with X-ray machines. A familiar panic started to rise in me, as I braced myself to not *râler*. Just as I was mustering the courage to stay calm, I heard a giggle—

it was Ana, chiming in from the passenger seat. "Oh, Max, stop teasing your mom!" And just like that, I realized Max had been pulling my leg again.

Lying there in bed, two hours into my *nuit blanche*, I found myself chuckling. What began as a night of frustration and worry had turned into one of laughter and perspective. Even my husband, sound asleep, snorted—a gentle reminder that, despite it all, life doesn't take itself too seriously.

"*Chéri, tu ronfles,*" I whispered, nudging him gently. He shifted, and I snuggled in closer, feeling the weight of the night slowly lift.

As my eyes began to close, a verse came to mind, etching tonight's lesson a little deeper into my heart: *Faites tout sans vous plaindre et sans discuter…et brillez comme des flambeaux dans le monde.* Do everything without complaining or arguing…and shine like beacons in the world.

FRENCH VOCABULARY

la nuit blanche
sleepless night

le cauchemar
nightmare

pouah!
ugh!

le téléphone portable
cell phone

Ouaf! Ouaf!
Woof! Woof!

le dodo
sleep (informal)

le sommeil
sleep

l'Hexagone (m)
A synonym for France, referencing its hexagonal shape

je râle
I complain

tout est impossible
everything is impossible

mais où est-elle
but where is she

bon
well

en retard
late

râler
to complain

chéri
darling (informal)

tu ronfles
you're snoring

Faites tout sans vous plaindre et sans discuter
Do everything without complaining or arguing

et brillez comme des flambeaux dans le monde
and shine like beacons in the world (Philippians 2:14-15)

33
VOILE

*I*t's the start of a new work week, and Jean-Marc, Ricci, and I have overslept. Perhaps Sunday's long luncheon at our new table, along with all the fantastic desserts our guests brought, weighed us down so much that we couldn't wake up on time.

"*Quelle heure est-il?*" my husband mumbles in the dark.

Below my feet, I can feel Ricci stretch as I reach for my phone. It's 6:51 a.m.

"*Je suis en retard!*" Jean-Marc gasps. I hurry downstairs to let our dog out and quickly make some *chicorée-café*, our new morning cup o' Joe as it is gentler on the nerves. Jean-Marc's phone is already ringing—harvesters at Domaine Antiane, the Bandol vineyard where he's in charge of *la vendange* this season, are arriving in the fields at sunrise. But which field? They want to know. It's amusing to imagine how my husband will give the precise coordinates to locate a specific block of *Mourvèdre* grapes. Will he say, "Just past the old windmill and over the creek? Turn left after the olive orchard…"? I can picture it now, having stumbled onto dozens of isolated parcels in the years we lived in the vineyards. Reaching to caress Ricci, I'm so grateful to be back in my warm bed, with my warm mug!

I leave Jean-Marc to deal with his vineyard dilemmas while I face my own: Which story should I write for this week's deadline?

Doubts swirl around the drafts forming in my mind. There's the one about my mom, tentatively titled "LaLa Land"—a place I suggest we all start dwelling more often, instead of taking everything so seriously. "These are the best days of our lives," I remind both Mom and myself, genuinely believing we should stop worrying about the who, what, where, and why—and once and for all step into this storybook life!

On the other hand, given this is Jackie's birth week (she's turning 27!), there's a funny anecdote about my daughter that I could write instead. She recently got me all worked up with her nearly impossible birthday plans: as she's beginning her master's program this week and would be away all day, she suggested we celebrate at 6:30 a.m. with pancakes, bacon, eggs, a fully decorated house, and the whole family in attendance. Just when I was about to unravel from all the detailed planning (and the pressure of trying to make it all perfect), she snickered, "Mom, I'm fine with a bowl of cereal. Relax!"

While I like both stories, I'm suddenly overwhelmed with doubt as I sip my coffee. Not only am I indecisive, but I'm also starting to worry that readers will tire of these same old anecdotes. After all, *c'est du pareil au même*—more of the same! Maybe I should be writing about sports, cryptocurrency, or *les actualités* instead…

As I sit there, panicking over my coffee, Jean-Marc calls up from the bottom of the stairwell, *"Bonne chance avec ton édition!"* He says that every time and, for a moment, I forget my fears. I think instead about the progress we've made and continue to make individually and as a couple. It's just a matter of staying the course… steady as she goes!

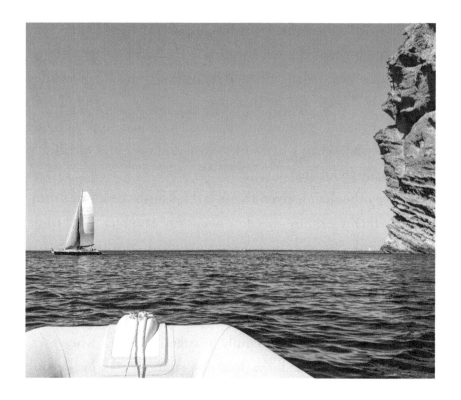

So far, this boat is sailing, even if, week after week, we get hit with our fair share of flotsam here on deck: a family crisis, a social conundrum, a traffic ticket, a plague of mites (thank God they finally disappeared). But when I stop and let the wind wash over me, I realize how freeing it is to face the gales head-on— *avec la foi.*

As one of my favorite French thinkers, François Fénelon, tutor to the Duke of Burgundy, once said, *"Le vent de Dieu souffle toujours; il vous faut seulement hisser la voile."* The wind of God is always blowing; you must only hoist your sail.

Though I didn't follow through with either story plan today, I managed to write—thanks in part to a certain Frenchman. Before rushing out into the vine fields, Jean-Marc took a moment to share a few uplifting words. What if, finally, that was the most important order of the day? Not to pick the right path, but to help hoist one another's sails?

As Ricci comes trotting back in from the yard, her nose wet from the morning dew, Jean-Marc's voice drifts in from the distance, where he's already absorbed in the vineyard's daily rhythm. I glance out the window and smile. The day is young, and with each other's support, we'll weather it—just as we've weathered all the others.

FRENCH VOCABULARY

la voile
sail

Quelle heure est-il?
What time is it?

Je suis en retard
I am late

le chicorée-café
chicory coffee

la vendange
the harvest

le Mourvèdre
Mourvèdre
(a type of grape)

**c'est du pareil
au même**
it's the same thing

les actualités
the news

**Bonne chance
avec ton édition**
Good luck with
your post

avec la foi
with faith

**Le vent de Dieu
souffle toujours;
il vous faut
seulement hisser
la voile**
The wind of God
is always blowing;
you must only
hoist the sail.

34
RAPLAPLA

This fall, my dog and I are in a competition to see who can lose the most hair. "I think you're winning," my hairdresser says, shaking more of my hair out of his hands.

"You should see my house," I laugh, "it's carpeted with fur! Maybe Ricci's winning?"

After some initial *plaisanteries*, I begin to close my eyes. I've finally made it to the salon, where I'll spend two hours trying to avoid eye contact with the woman in the mirror. I don't like *la cicatrice* on her forehead, and her cheeks have tiny red veins I know are there, even if I've covered them with *fond de teint*. And though I carefully washed it a day before (my hairdresser doesn't like a greasy scalp) my hair is limp and stringy. There's an amusing French word for this not-so-amusing condition of flat and lifeless locks: *raplapla*.

Too bad *raplapla* is wasted on lifeless locks because it would make a fine interjection—as it always takes a bit of oomph to drag me out of my nest and into this swivel chair, especially during *l'heure de la sieste*. Why is it that hair appointments and Amazon deliveries always seem to fall during these most delectable hours?

"*Les mèches et une coupe, s'il vous plaît*"... The last time I phoned the salon for these was three months ago for a wedding. Three

months before that, a trip with my best friend was my motivation to *aller chez le coiffeur*. And before that, it was my 56th birthday. A grand total of four trips a year—and if it weren't for these social occasions, it would be even fewer, and I'd go around with my hair tied back and covered in a hat for as long as I could get away with it.

I hear door chimes and look up from my swivel chair. A couple walks in. *Bonjour, Messieurs Dames*, they say, greeting a room full of clients in various stages of transformation. With no more available chairs in this tiny salon, the man settles in at *l'espace shampoing*. *How lovely to come to the salon together!* I think, studying the sweethearts, each in shoes with Velcro closures. I make a mental note to bring my surefooted husband next time—but there's no way Jean-Marc would wait two hours in a room full of fancy lotions and potions. Give him a field of musky grapes and some *sécateurs*, and he'd cut his own hair if he could—and dye it purple with *le jus de raisin*.

My eyes water from the toxic fumes of peroxide as Cyril begins the technique known as *le balayage*, painting thick white cream onto another lock of my hair and wrapping each section in plastic. I look away from the thinning mop he's working on and ask about his recent trip to Corsica.

C'était merveilleux! Le fromage Corse, les saucissons, les cascades, les piscines naturelles—and you can take your dog with you everywhere!

I think about my upcoming trip with Dad and my sisters. We'll meet in Barcelona for a Mediterranean cruise…including a stop in Corsica. Imagine being able to take my dog—that would be heaven! Just as *Le Paradis* is paved in gold, our ship would be paved in platinum—tufts and tufts of it, both Ricci's and mine!

I smile at the thought and glance around the salon. More customers have arrived with thinning hair and graying roots. The creases and scars on our faces reflect experiences, adventure, and a quiet confidence that, in spite of our collective *raplapla*—our limp and lifeless locks—life is full! I look back at the woman in the mirror. This time, she has a pleasant smile. The critical gaze is gone. We are all the same, really. In our day-to-day lives, we're all just trying to keep our hair on.

FRENCH VOCABULARY

raplapla
limp or lifeless

la plaisanterie
joke, banter

la cicatrice
scar

le fond de teint
fondation
(makeup)

**l'heure (f)
de la sieste**
nap time

les mèches (f)
highlights

la coupe
cut

s'il vous plaît
please

**aller chez le
coiffeur**
to go to the
hairdresser

**Bonjour,
Messieurs Dames**
Hello, ladies and
gentlemen

**l'espace
shampoing (m)**
shampoo station

le sécateur
pruning shears

le jus de raisin
grape juice

le balayage
a hair coloring
technique with
hand-painted
highlights

C'était merveilleux
It was wonderful

le fromage corse
Corsican cheese

le saucisson
dried sausage

la cascade
waterfall

la piscine naturelle
natural
swimming pool

le Paradis
Paradise

OCTOBER

Octobre

35
PAPA CHÉRI

*I*t's 4:15 a.m., and I've just hugged my sister, Heidi, goodbye. She is on her way home to Denver. In another three hours, it will be time to send off our other sister, Kelley, and our dad, who will fly back to Seattle. We have just spent nine days together, laughing, reminiscing, and toasting to this collective effort to be together once again—and the sunny Mediterranean was the ideal backdrop for our family reunion at sea!

After our dad launched the idea of a father-daughter voyage a few years ago, it was our little sister who tracked down the ideal seven-day *séjour*. Kelley, a flight attendant, learned about Azamara cruises thanks to her colleague Susie, who is experienced in *les croisières*. Being cruise novices, we weren't sure what to expect, but since our goal was to spend time together and celebrate Dad's upcoming 83rd birthday, we didn't really care about perfection—though that's exactly what we got! Our Mediterranean itinerary began in Spain and stopped at ports along the south of France. While it may seem strange to go port-hopping so close to home (Collioure, Marseille, Toulon, Sanary-sur-Mer, Nice, Monaco—and even Ajaccio are familiar spots), I appreciated my family's willingness to travel in my direction. My dad was hesitant but agreed to traverse three international airports, security,

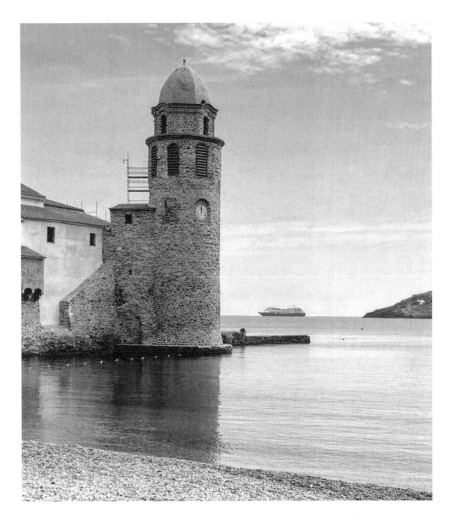

customs, and the rest. He was accompanied all the way by a first-class flight attendant—Kelley—which made the deal a little sweeter.

There in Barcelona, before boarding Azamara's 700-passenger ship, Onward, my sister Heidi and I waited our turn in line to check our bags. Ahead of us stood a tall, beautiful blonde and a distinguished gentleman who could have been her father. That's because he was her father—only onlookers could easily make the wrong assumption! We needed to have T-shirts printed to clear up any confusion. One would read "That's my Dad" (with a large arrow) and the other, "That's my daughter —>." On second thought, why not have Dad's T-shirt read "Sugar Daddy" and give those accidental gawkers something to gossip about! Given the range of characters aboard our ship, there was no shortage of misconceptions, and we enjoyed every minute of people-watching—and making our own colorful conclusions.

After checking our bags and going through security, we boarded the cruise ship and headed straight to lunch, poolside. Incidentally, poolside would be the only part of the ship we'd easily recognize, as we never did figure out exactly where we were on the 181-meter-long, multi-storied vessel. To borrow a line from our sister, "Passengers tend to check their brains with their bags…" Kelley means that tenderly, as that's what vacation is all about: relaxing the mind.

With seven days ahead of us, we had plenty of time to orient ourselves. Though I still can't tell you whether these places were bow, starboard, port, or stern side, here are the spots we frequented most: the Cabaret Room (for evening entertainment, including Disco Night and Bingo), the Den (for the piano bar), the walking/jogging track for daily exercise (and a spectacular early morning view of the latest port), the library, and the various eateries.

Every morning, we began with breakfast at Windows Café. The selection was vast—from *le saumon fumé* to pancakes—it was, as the French say, *l'embarras du choix*, overwhelming! Each night we dined at Discoveries Restaurant, and it was as good as the fine dining (five floors up) we experienced the first night. Lobster, *filet mignon*, crab cakes, lamb…the selection was *gastronomique*. Every-

thing was cooked to order and delicious. Located near two onboard boutiques, the Mosaic Café was my favorite stop for a twice-daily latté and *les gourmandises* (cookies, carrot cake, lemon tart). There was even an array of dainty tea sandwiches. Ordering whatever you desire felt like being Charlie in The Chocolate Factory. On this cruise ship, everything is included—even *le pourboire*! My conscience was rattled at every meal, but the waiters insisted waste was dealt with ecologically (if not geographically. In a perfect world all the untouched food would be packed up and delivered fresh to the ports for immediate redistribution).

Our room being located above the bow, we were shaken awake that first morning by the lowering of a massive anchor! We

dressed, had breakfast, and took a tender off the boat to reach our first destination: Port Vendres. Just in front of the tourist office, we stepped onto *Le Petit Train*, heading towards Collioure. The weather was so sunny and warm, people were swimming in the sparkling cove—in October!

We made it back to the boat for lunch and a little siesta, followed by drinks and dinner. We repeated this agreeable schedule daily (except in Marseille, where we met up with Jackie for a private shopping tour and lunch near *Le Vieux Port*. Aunt Heidi and Aunt Kelley were delighted to see their *nièce*, but Grandpa stayed on the boat, nursing a slight cold. He would gladly catch up with his granddaughter later in the week).

As for catching up, on this trip my sisters were on a sentimental mission: to make up for lost time. Heidi and I grew up in the Arizona desert, while Kelley was born and raised in Washington State. Beginning when Kelley was a teenager, we three gathered whenever possible, but geographical distance made it challenging. Now, in mid-life, here we were, together again and taking enough pictures to crash our dad's phone. We may not have a family picture or Christmas card from bygone days but, *ouistiti!* there was no stopping us now.

"Here, let me help you with your hair," Heidi said one evening, offering me a salon-worthy blowout. She had this amazing brush and, after enough hints, she gifted it to me just to shut me up! Like teenagers, we shared each other's stuff and savoir-faire, as siblings do. Kelley offered us each a *trousse de toilette*, filled with lotions and potions and we all giggled when Dad chimed in, telling us how much he enjoyed the eye mask. We had to give Dad credit for managing to participate in all our girly conversations, though he drew the line at window shopping, or "*lécher les vitrines*" as the French say (literally "licking windows"). We could spend hours in antique stores and boutiques at every port.

During the cruise, we each reveled in one-on-one time with Dad. While my sisters enjoyed father-daughter conversations on the sundeck, I relished our indoor *tête-à-têtes*, always tender and *amusants*. Over coffee with Dad at the Mosaic Café, we were talking about tap water when Dad casually mentioned he was drinking from the bathroom sink in his cabin. "Dad!" I cautioned, "You can't do that!"

"Sure I can. I drink tap water all the time."

I called the *barista* over to explain why this was a bad idea, given how much bleach they use to treat seawater. Dad allowed the young man to elaborate before replying, "Well, it may have some imperfection…but it's not poisonous imperfection! I'll stick to the cabin water!"

Speaking of cabins—or "staterooms"—Dad and Kelley shared one with twin beds, while Heidi and I were one floor below in a near-identical layout. Everything was comfortable except the temperature…and so began the thermostat wars. My sisters, with their Antarctic leanings, would've been better climate companions for each other. Dad and I prefer heat, so when the girls were sleeping, we turned up the dials!

One night, on our way up to the Atlas Bar on the 10th floor for our evening *apéro*—"Parisians" (champagne cocktails) for them, Perrier for *moi*—an elegant couple entered the elevator. Dad, captivated by the woman's beaded jacket, flashed me a mischievous look before swiping at a string of dangling beads on the back. Unbeknownst to the glamorous fashionista and her civilized companion, the beads swayed innocently. I almost died!

"Dad!!!" was our not-so-indignant response to every mischievous word or deed coming from our *papa chéri*.

One particularly poignant evening balanced out these daily shenanigans. Over dinner, we asked Dad about his time in the Air Force, when we were with him in the Philippines, after he married Mom and adopted Heidi. He told us very little about the Vietnam War, but his visible sadness spoke volumes. As we quietly contemplated Dad's words, a passenger from a nearby table appeared. "Thank you, Sir, for your service," she said, simply. There followed a cosmic lull: time stood still. Next thing I knew my sisters had tears in their eyes. I felt a ball form in my throat imagining the full impact of war—on those targeted and those sent out to target others. Glancing over at Dad, I saw tears in his eyes for the first time.

In addition to so many tragic losses, there was the fallout among families, too. As Kelley dried her tears, I reminded her of something our Mom (Heidi's and mine) often says when we feel sadness about the breakup of our family. According to Jules, "If it wasn't for the divorce, we would have never gotten our precious Kelley!" (who toddled joyfully into this world after Dad remarried and who, all grown up now, became our compass on this trip, handling all the logistics and guiding us through the ports).

That emotional night brought a tender closeness to the rest of our *chanceux* father-daughter journey. As we disembarked from the ship, we felt a wave of gratitude for the way this time together had fortified our family ties. The sunny ports of the Mediterranean were enchanting, but it was the shared stories, laughter, and meaningful moments with Dad that made our trip shine. We raise our glasses to those memories, now, *Tchin! Tchin!*—and to our *papa chéri*.

POST NOTE: *Papa chéri* in French translates to "sweet dad." You might say our would-be Sugar Daddy T-shirts are fitting after all! :-)

FRENCH VOCABULARY

papa chéri
sweet Dad,
darling Dad

le séjour
stay

la croisière
cruise

le saumon fumé
smoked salmon

**l'embarras (m)
du choix**
too many choices

le filet mignon
fine cut of beef

gastronomique
gourmet

la gourmandise
treats

le pourboire
tip

Le Petit Train
The Little Train

le Vieux Port
the Old Port

la nièce
niece

ouistiti!
say cheese!

**la trousse
de toilette**
toiletry kit

lécher les vitrines
window shopping
(literally "lick the
windows")

le tête-à-tête
one-on-one
conversation

amusants (mpl)
funny

le barista
a person who
serves coffee
in a coffee bar

l'apéro (m)
pre-dinner drink

moi
me

chanceux
lucky

tchin! tchin!
cheers

LAQUELLE

Laquelle? That is the question of the day! With so many things happening each week, picking just one incident to write about can be a real *casse-tête*.

Should I title this one *Grand-mère Chérie* and talk about the blessings of our *aînés*? Especially the French grandmother who warmed to Ricci and me while we were shopping for greens. Entering the *maraîcher's*, the only other client in the tiny shop approached. "What a lovely dog!" she began. By the time our conversation was over, I knew exactly which *champignons* to buy (not those from *Haute-Savoie*—too gorged with liquid—wait another week, and the local *chanterelles* will be in stock). "Do you like *nougat*?" my new friend continued. "They make it just over the hill from Ceyreste—in Signes…" And there I thought *nougat* was from Montélimar, only, and that *signes* was French for monkey (just kidding—that would be *singes*).

Putting geography and nougat aside for a moment (that last one will take willpower, *n'est-ce pas?*)…and back to our *l'embarras du choix:* I could write instead about Jean-Marc's latest Provence Wine Tour. What a treat to meet Donna, Jim, and Nancy over coffee at *Le Rose Thé* hotel here in La Ciotat. "We feel like we know you," Donna shared, having read this blog for years. The

feeling was mutual. Whether it was *l'alchimie* or sudden *camara-derie*, this encounter felt like reconnecting with old friends. After coffee, Donna's husband, Jim, agreed to drive us to the world-re-nowned *Château de Pibarnon*, in the verdant hills above Bandol, then on to Cassis, to *Domaine du Paternel*. From Bandol's hilltops to Cassis' cliffs (*falaises*) and the hairpin turns in between, we were glad Jim was behind the wheel. Jean-Marc, our copilot, filled us in on the sights, adding a little history along the way. It felt good to get our feet back on solid ground as we strolled through colorful Cassis after lunch on the port at *Le Bar de la Marine*. But not for long. We lifted off, once again, to reach the heights of *La Route des Crêtes*, where behind us the valley was carpeted with purple heather, and before us, a long way down the cliff, the turquoise blue sea spread out to infinity. I could go on about our picturesque *périple*, but back to our story-choice dilemma...

Maybe you're curious to read about the monumental tongue-lashing Ricci and I received while sneaking across the beach, and the Ice Queen out in the frigid sea, hollering at me. During the off-season, their backyard having been battered all summer by tourists, the locals wander out to the empty beaches, often with their dogs. What a pleasure to see all the neighbor-hood *chiens*, bouncing and rollicking among the rocks and sand.

Normally, groups of people walk in the cold, shallow waters each morning, even in late fall. It is invigorating, wonderful exercise—and mood-lifting. But not for all....

"Get your dog off this beach!" The goggle-eyed woman thun-dered, stomping through the water. "It's disgusting. All the crap they leave is full of disease. *Allez! Va-t'en!* Get out of here!" I don't know what crap she is referring to as I have rarely seen it on the beach (though there is plenty of human-generated litter…).

"Come on, Ricci!" I tugged at the leash, where a half dozen neon-pink doggie waste bags were tied at the ready (offered by the city—the pink is for *Octobre Rose*, breast cancer month). In addition to picking up after our dogs, we often pick up litter, giving those free bags extra duty.

During the woman's tirade, Ricci dug her feet in, intent to do her business then and there… *Oh no! Not here!* Just when I began sweating it—the fear, the condemnation, the public humiliation… *plot twist!* A crowd at the café began yelling back at the ice queen, "*Ferme ta gueule!* Shut up!" Caught in the crossfire, Ricci and I tiptoed off the battlefield…and hurried home to tell Mama Jules everything. "That's why I stay in bed," Mom smiled. "Because, this time of day, all the nuts come out!"

Ouf! I'm tired just thinking about which story to expand upon. Wait a minute, there's one more! I could write about that surreal wait, Monday, *chez le gynéco*, where everyone behaved like they were on the Paris Métro: not daring to look at each other lest they break some supernatural law. There in the waiting room, I found myself wondering what brought each woman here. Some were obvious—a pregnant belly here, perhaps birth control pills there…and as for us three middle-aged *nanas: prolapsus? Incontinence? Menopause? All three? (*Yes! But one doesn't talk about such things! Just like on the Paris Métro, where you mustn't look into a stranger's eyes, certain subjects are best left *unexamined*.)

Enfin, voilà! Every week it's the same dilemma: which slice of life to share? So many stories, each has its drama, suspense, and even its own moral. But which one to write about? *Laquelle?* And therein lies the hitch: whether you're a writer or a dreamer, you've got to choose a path today and ride it out to the end. *Vroom! Vroom!* After all, the journey is what makes each tale worth telling, each dream worth dreaming, and each day worth living.

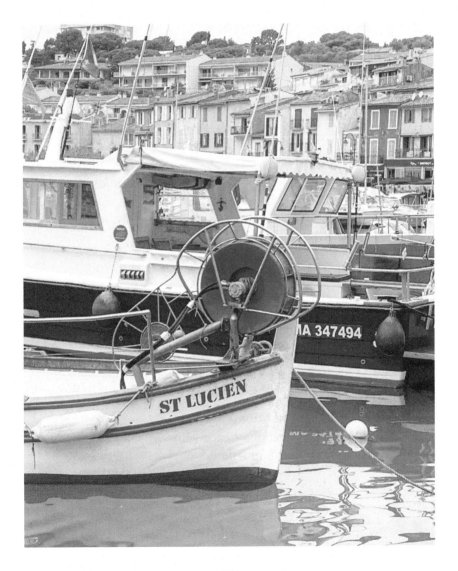

FRENCH VOCABULARY

laquelle
which, which one

le casse-tête
the puzzle

la grand-mère
the grandmother

chéri(e)
dear, sweet

les aîné(e)s (f)
the elders

le maraîcher
the greengrocer

les champignons (m)
the mushrooms

la Haute-Savoie
the Haute-Savoie

la chanterelle
chanterelle (golden
wild mushroom,
fragrant and tasty)

Signes
a small village
in the Provençal
hinterland

le singe
monkey

n'est-ce pas
isn't that true?

**l'embarras (m)
du choix**
overwhelming
options

Le Rose Thé
tea room whose
name means
"pink tea"

l'alchimie (f)
the chemistry

la camaraderie (f)
feeling of friendship
and fellowship

les falaises (f)
the cliffs

le périple
journey

le chien
dog

Allez! Va-t'en!
Go! Get out of here!

Octobre rose
pink October,
to mark breast
cancer awareness

ferme ta gueule!
shut your mouth!

ouf!
whew!

chez le gynéco
at the gynecologist's

les nanas
women
(informal, slang)

enfin, voilà
so there you have it

37
ESSAYER

Twenty-two years ago, on a crisp autumn morning, the scent of candy in the air, this blog was born. In the medieval village of Les Arcs-sur-Argens, preparations were underway for Halloween—a totally new concept in France at the time. A ghoulish parade was about to begin, with local children dressed as witches, ghosts, skeletons, and little devils, going door to door to collect *bonbons* from village merchants, while *des citrouilles d'Halloween* flickered on porches, illuminating the festive spirit. There in the municipal parking lot, amidst a crowd of novice trick-or-treaters, my five-year-old Jackie and her seven-year-old *frérot* were giddy, and so was I…

That Halloween parade was my first cultural event to report on, and I covered the entire subject in one brief entry in this online journal. Here's an excerpt from October 31, 2002:

> *Guess what? The French are celebrating Halloween! Today children will* se défiler *(parade) down the village streets dressed as* sorcières *(witches),* fantômes *(ghosts), and* citrouilles *(pumpkins). In France, the citizens haven't yet figured out that it's okay to be Elvis for Halloween…* Les enfants *(the children) will* solliciter *local bakeries, butchers, and various shops for candy (*bonbons*).*

Granted, that short *billet* was more of a headline than a story. But soon, these paragraph-long reports grew into soulful *essais*—and how fitting that word is, coming from the verb *essayer* (to try). I soon learned that all you needed to be a writer was the willingness to *essayer*—the courage to try.

Since that day, I've been an essayist. And, remarkably, it's no easier today than it was 22 years ago, which sometimes baffles me. But then, that's true of every worthy pursuit, isn't it? As you progress you build experience but, just like jumping off a cliff, the fall is never shorter. You may have better gear, more wisdom, and more muscle, but that doesn't eliminate the fear, the risk of rejection from publishers and readers, and the looming threat of humiliation. Because once you have got your story down, no matter your intention, *interpretation* is out of your control. All you can do is try to improve your expression, day after day after day. Then one day, you repost an essay from years ago—only to get this feedback: "Loved today's story! Your writing has improved so much!"

Maybe we don't get better. But we get bolder!

Back to the grind… Each day brings the challenge of not knowing what to write about—in this blog post, in that magazine column, in this upcoming chapter—whatever the pen-worthy assignment might be. It can feel as daunting as a skeleton lurking in the closet, a goblin staring you down, or as unnerving as a ghostly whisper of doubt. And that brings us to today: Halloween! Just what is there left to say *about that?* Should I wax poetic about mums? During *Toussaint,* chrysanthemums are the French flower of choice for cemeteries—*precisely why you should never bring them as a hostess gift*! Or perhaps I could describe the decorations that've gone up in town, in orange and black—so many pumpkins, spiders, and bats! Or let me tell you about the stash of candy I've amassed for the four trick-or-treaters who'll hopefully ring our doorbell after sundown. Currently, *les friandises* are hidden from Jean-Marc, though I know our sweets thief will end up with them all tomorrow—when he'll split *le butin* with his bewitching *belle-mère* Jules. Just don't share with Ricci—chocolate is poisonous for dogs! Instead, we'll offer her the pumpkin-themed jellybeans.

Voilà, my stab at a Halloween report—or *essai*—this year. Time, now, to figure out how to close this birthday post disguised as a spooky story…

On this, *l'anniversaire* of *French Word-A-Day*, I'd like to express my heartfelt gratitude. *Merci beaucoup,* dear reader, for lining up outside my door, like the most faithful trick-or-treater, waiting to see what goodies are in store for you today. I wouldn't be here, all dressed up in my Writer costume, if it weren't for you showing up on the other side of this portal. And now here we are together, many Halloweens later! Max and Jackie are all grown up and will greet trick-or-treaters *chez eux.* So many changes in your lives, too. Yet through it all, we continue on—writer and reader—for as long as we can say "*bêtise ou friandise*," Trick or Treat! Ultimately, while writing may be fraught with uncertainty, it is also filled with countless blessings, reminding us that every word penned is a gift shared between writer and reader.

FRENCH VOCABULARY

essayer
to try

Les Arcs-sur-Argens
a medieval village in Provence

le bonbon

candy

la citrouille d'Halloween
jack-o-lantern

le frérot
kid brother

se défiler
to parade

la sorcière
witch

le fantôme
ghost

la citrouille
pumpkin

les enfants (m)
children

solliciter
to solicit

le billet
short article

l'essai (m)
essay

la Toussaint
All Saints' Day

la friandise
candy

le butin
loot

la belle-mère
mother-in-law
(also: stepmother)

voilà
so there you have it

l'anniversaire (m)
anniversary,
birthday

merci beaucoup
thanks so much

chez eux
at their place

bêtise ou friandise
Trick or Treat

NOVEMBER

Novembre

NOVEMBER

38

KINÉ

When my mobile phone rang, I picked up to hear a sunny voice on the other end. "Hey, Mom. Want to have lunch together at the port?"

"Hi, Max! I would have loved to, but I have an appointment at *la kiné*! And hey, next time you go to St. Tropez, take me along," I said, remembering his wine delivery there yesterday.

My son laughed. "Next time!"

I said goodbye, gathered *ma carte Vitale, mes clés, et mes lunettes*, and set off to my physical therapist's office. I enjoyed the walk, which took me through our neighborhood, past the local *lycée* and across a municipal park. There, nestled among a cluster of apartment buildings, was the only medical *cabinet* in an otherwise residential space. Above the entrance, a fluffy orange cat stretched on a balcony beside some hanging laundry drying in the sun. I punched in the key code, made my way past several private apartments, and entered the cozy setup, which felt more like a friend's living room than a clinic.

"*Bonjour*," my *kiné* said, greeting me with a pair of bats perched humorously on her head—a funny contrast, given the serious demeanor French healthcare workers typically maintain. A moment later, two dogs dressed as goblins trotted over. Hector, a

Border Collie mix, and Maika, a Cavalier King Charles, wagged their *queues* as they greeted me. Once they recognized the patient, they settled back into their respective beds beneath the therapy table where I now rested.

My *kiné* studied the graph on the screen beside her, instructing me when to relax and contract. *Respirez…Serrez…respirez…serrez.*" And so began another 20-minute session to "re-educate *le périnée*"…

In France, when a woman gives birth, she's offered—courtesy of the French healthcare system—ten sessions of physical therapy with a *kinésithérapeute* to help her recover. But back when I had Max, at the age of 27, new to France, I didn't understand what *rééducation périnéale* was, let alone what it entailed. And with a baby to care for, I skipped it altogether. Now, thirty years later, I regret that decision—a choice I was reminded of on our recent family cruise when a mini health crisis sent me straight from the ship to the doctor's office.

As I lay there, feeling the device contract my muscles, I winced. It wasn't intolerable, but it wasn't *sans douleur* either. I breathed out, relaxing, when the soft snoring from one of the dogs helped lull me into a reverie.

My mind drifted to memories of other atypical healthcare offices in France…like the dentist's in Lille. Back in 1989, during a university exchange program in the north of France, *un mal de dents* sent me to the neighborhood tooth slayer. I remember setting out after dark for my 6:30 p.m. appointment—an unusual time for a dental procedure by American standards. But that wasn't the only surprise. When I rang the bell, I was startled to be at a private home.

"*Bonjour*," a man said, and just as I was about to respond, in elementary French, that I must have the wrong address. "*Entrez*," he said, gesturing me inside.

I followed the older man past a dining room, where a table was set for dinner. There was even a bottle of wine on the table and everywhere, antique furniture. In the back, lights glowed in the kitchen, illuminating a woman cooking at the stove. The aroma of stewed meat made me salivate—dinner in France was much later than back home. Soon I'd return to my host family's for another delicious meal that Madame Bassimon was cooking. But not before the dentist—if that's who this was—treated my toothache. Just where was that going to happen? *Dans la cuisine?*

Le monsieur of a certain age creaked open a door just off the living room, revealing an exam room complete with a reclining chair. "*Asseyez-vous,*" he gestured. I sat back and stared nervously at *le plafond.* Back home in Phoenix, my dentist's ceiling was covered in cartoons and humorous images, a distraction to keep patients relaxed. Here in Lille, in this ancient building, the ceiling was also plastered—but with ornate, centuries-old moldings that were equally distracting. My eyes traced the swirling lines when suddenly I heard the drill and the command, "*Ouvrez la bouche!*" But the dentist had not given me a shot to numb the area. Just what kind of dentist was this? Help! *Au secours!!*

Back in the present, at my *kiné's* office in La Ciotat, the sound of "the drill from Lille" fades into a soft snore as I wake from my reverie to the hum of *ronflements.* Two furry goblins beneath the PT table stir on hearing the familiar words. "*Ça va? Tout va bien?*" The session was over.

I looked up at the woman with the bats on her head. "*Oui, ça va. Merci.* Everything was fine—just as it had been at the dentist's all those years ago." Somehow, getting a tooth filled without Novocain was possible, just as it's possible for a healthcare office in France to feel as familiar as home. There's a certain charm to that, and maybe—just maybe—it's this charm that takes the edge off the pain.

FRENCH VOCABULARY

le/la kiné
short for kinésithérapeute, physical therapist

la carte vitale
health insurance card

la clé
key

les lunettes
eyeglasses

le lycée
high school

le cabinet
doctor's office

Bonjour
hello

la queue
tail

respirez
breathe

serrez
squeeze, tighten

le périnée
perineum, pelvic muscle

le/la kinésithérapeute
physical therapist

la rééducation périnéale
perineal re-education, pelvic floor therapy

sans douleur
without pain

un mal de dents
toothache

Entrez
come in

dans la cuisine
in the kitchen

le Monsieur
the man

Asseyez-vous
sit down

le plafond
ceiling

Ouvrez la bouche
open your mouth

Au secours!
Help!

le ronflement
snore

Ça va?
Are you okay?

Tout va bien?
Is everything okay?

Oui
yes

Merci
thank you

39
LOUCHE

Jean-Marc and I had been looking forward to celebrating our 30th anniversary for months. This belated trip to Italy, with its promise of rest, renewal, et *de bons repas*, seemed like the perfect way to mark the occasion. But as we landed in Bari just past midnight, the excitement was quickly replaced by a chill in the air and an unsettling *obscurité*.

It was cold and dark as we stood at the airport taxi stand among a crowd of travelers. Just like with the French, there was no rhyme or reason to the *queue*. After a few moments, Jean-Marc cleared his throat and asked the couple next to us, "Have you been waiting long?"

Just as we began to question the apparent lack of taxis, a man stepped out from the shadows and approached us. Something about him seemed *louche*, his voice low and measured as he asked, "Need a ride?"

"How much will it cost?" Jean-Marc ventured. And just like that, we, along with the other couple, followed the stranger. The young woman ahead of me carried a backpack. I followed, carting my *valise*, while our partners trailed behind. We continued to the end of the sidewalk, beyond the airport's railway station. As we got further and further from the terminal, I turned to whisper to the

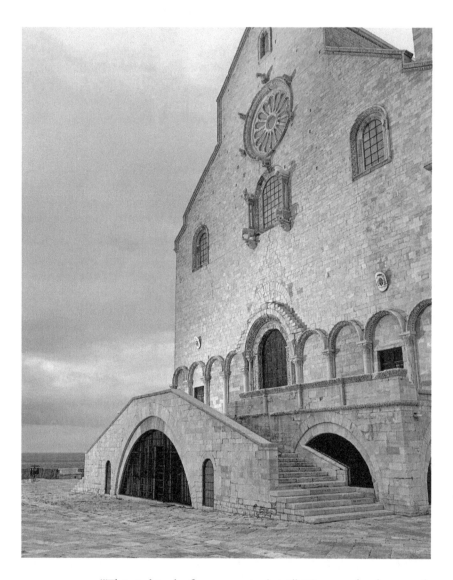

young man, "This is kind of strange, isn't it?" He merely shrugged. With no Uber service available in Bari, what other choice did we have for getting to the town center after midnight?

When we arrived at the rental car lot, I felt a moment of relief. Surely, one of those official cars must be ours. *Hélas*, our driver quickly bypassed the rentals, heading instead toward a chain-link fence and out of the airport grounds, casting frequent glances over his shoulder to ensure we were following.

The young woman slowed her steps. "Look, this is…I don't…" she began.

"I don't like this either!" I hissed to Jean-Marc, my nerves prickling.

"It's around the corner," the driver piped in, urging us forward. Incredibly, we followed, like sheep heading to an uncertain fate. If I went along, it was because I trusted my husband. But that didn't mean he always made the safest decisions… Years ago, during a hike along the rocky seaside he suggested a shortcut along the train tracks *through a narrow tunnel.* This dark path we were on now felt just as chilling. *When would the ominous "train" appear and crush us?*

The silence of the night, the scraping, churning wheels of our suitcases became the soundtrack to a Hitchcock scene. The so-called driver appeared nervous. My mind reeled when he suddenly spoke. "Where are you going?"

Yes, that was my question!

"The Boston Hotel," Jean-Marc answered before the stranger could read my thoughts.

"Uh, we're going to an Airbnb," the young man replied.

A fleeting, guilty thought crossed my mind: *I hoped we would be dropped off first.* I didn't want to be The Last Stop. The Terminus. *The Terminated…*

C'est chelou! This is bizarre! Just where *was* this "cab"? After what seemed like a mile, we turned into a dark alley. There it was: a battered station wagon the French refer to as *un break*—as in a *prison break*. There was no taxi dome light on the roof, no company logo on the doors, no meter inside—not even a GPS. And there was virtually no room for all our suitcases. Something screamed SKETCHY.

Before we could ask questions, the stranger hoisted the young woman's suitcase onto one of the seats. "OK, ok. Let's go." I quickly got in, picking up the suitcase and placing it on my lap.

"I'm not doing this!" the young woman declared, grabbing her luggage. Next the couple hurried off. I watched as what might be our only witnesses in this kidnapping disappeared.

Quit overreacting! Sheesh. You've watched too many scary episodes of Dateline. I tried to brush off my fears. But still, the thought did cross my mind—what if this wasn't quite as it seemed? What if we were about to be trafficked? Then again, I couldn't imagine us being the prime targets. I mean, who would go through the trouble of kidnapping a couple of middle-aged tourists?

Thinking about it now, it seems strange that Jean-Marc got into the front seat. Perhaps he felt more in control? As the car disappeared into the night, I fumbled for my phone, needing to turn the data back on to verify we were on our way to the Boston Hotel and not to some barren field on the outskirts of the city.

Come on, come on! I tried to locate the data button. Settings… Cellular…Roaming… There! I typed in "Boston Hotel," and the blue line appeared like a lifeline. Slightly relieved, I remained on guard. Just because the driver began chatting about tourist attractions didn't mean he wasn't planning something sinister.

From the backseat, I studied his profile. You might say he was good-looking, in a Ted Bundy kind of way—*pas vilain, ce vilain.* But you can't judge a book by its cover. I sank deeper into my projected horror story as the two men in front talked like tomorrow was certain. Would it be?

"What are your plans?" the driver asked. Jean-Marc mentioned we would be heading back to the airport to pick up our rental car, to which the driver casually replied, "Will you need a ride?"

There was a pause. *My husband wasn't seriously considering that, was he?*

Bright city lights came into view. We were only a few kilometers away. And then...the driver missed the turn-off. *Qu'est-ce qui se passe?* My pulse quickened, but at the next corner, we were back on track. Finally, there it was—the brightly lit *Boston Hotel* sign. What a funny name for a hotel in Southern Italy. Never mind! It might as well have been an American flag or the Statue of Liberty. I let out a long, shaky sigh, as if being repatriated from a battle zone, a war in my mind.

As we handed over our passports to the hotel clerk, Jean-Marc glanced at me with an amused smile that said, *Tu vois. Tout s'est bien passé.* I managed a laugh, a mix of relief and disbelief.

As for our driver, he no longer looked like a criminal in my mind, but a father or son or brother—a family man working a graveyard shift to make ends meet. While this was probably closer to the truth, it doesn't mean I'll ever step into an unmarked cab again, in a foreign city, after dark.

FRENCH VOCABULARY

louche
shady, suspicious

de
some

bon
good

le repas
meal(s)

l'obscurité
darkness

la queue
line

la valise
suitcase

hélas
alas

chelou
bizarre, shady

le break
station wagon

pas vilain, ce vilain
not bad
for a bad guy

**Qu'est-ce
qui se passe?**
What is happening?

Tu vois
you see

**Tout s'est bien
passé**
everything went
well

40
CRÉMAILLÈRE

1er Coup de Clé: On vous attend ce soir à 20 h pour notre premier coup de clé dans notre nouvel appartement.

The WhatsApp message read: "First Turn of the Key: We're expecting you tonight at 8pm for our first turn of the key in our new apartment."

This was more than just an invitation—it was a milestone for Max and Ana. After several years together, this young couple had taken the next big step: buying a nest to call their own. For Jean-Marc and me, it was deeply moving to witness this commitment, a tangible sign of their journey and their shared dreams.

We were excited to see their new home, nestled just a few kilometers from Max's previous apartment, closer to the foothills of La Ciotat and the famous, winding *Route des Crêtes*. This scenic road, flanked by purple *bruyère* fading to deep amber as the months grow colder, offered a hint of the charm in the new chapter Max and Ana were beginning.

Huddled in front of an open *fenêtre*, ice-cold air chilling our faces, we listened to Max as he continued our tour of the couple's new digs.

"Here in the *chambre d'amis*, you can see the green hills in the distance—during the day, that is."

Looking out into the night sky, the scene was poetic: a full moon peeking through the clouds and the neighborhood below illuminated like a painting. A dark green *pin parasol* hinted at where we were in France—here near the Mediterranean Sea. "You can see it from the balcony," my son added. For Max, just like for his father, the sea, with its nearby islands to sail to, its prickly *oursins* to catch and savor, and its familiar maritime scent, was an essential part of his habitat, given he was born near the coast and its rocky *calanques*. If, some 29 years ago, his first scent had been the rose petals his grandmother picked for him outside the maternity clinic, the next thing to tickle his nostrils was the salty sea air in Marseille!

"It's wonderful," I said. "The place has good bones!" Looking around, the walls were bare, exposing wiring, holes, and other secrets hidden behind the furniture the previous owners removed before their *déménagement*. From the looks of it, Max and Ana had a sizable renovation ahead of them, but from the sparkle in their eyes as they showed us around it was clear they were up for the challenge. *Même pas peur!* as the natives say.

Ana shared her plans for the following day: *"Je vais attaquer le papier peint."* While Max returned to work, Ana would be single-handedly removing all the wallpaper—*in the dark* as the electric shutters would be accidentally closed after tonight's party (when the couple returned to their current apartment, so tired, they forgot about the electricity being temporarily shut off the next day, owing to a change in contracts).

The echo of our voices in the empty apartment, the pitter-patter of scratchy dog paws, and the tap tap tapping of our heels gave the space a lively, festive feel. But I couldn't help wondering if

the neighbor downstairs could hear it all. Would they complain about the noisy celebration? I hoped this spirited start wouldn't get things off on the wrong foot with *les voisins*.

Thankfully, the younger generation doesn't worry as much as I do. Everything fascinates them, *especially human potential*. "The woman above us on the 4th floor is 92 years old," Max shared, raising his glass for the toast. "There's no elevator, and she climbs the stairs at least once a day—whether or not she has errands to run."

By the way, in France, what Americans call the 5th floor is referred to as the 4th floor. In the UK and other countries, where the ground floor is followed by the first floor, this system will feel more familiar. In France, the ground level is called the rez-de-chaussée (ground floor), making the first floor the one above it. It's helpful to know when navigating French buildings—or climbing stairs!

I could just picture the sprightly nonagenarian and her daily *aller-retour* on the central staircase. I love these examples of gumption and fortitude, whether from the venerable, like the 92-year-old upstairs, or the young, like Ana, who can't wait to make a dent in this renovation with a sledgehammer.

Making our way back through the hallway, we found a lively *crémaillère* underway. My brother-in-law Jacques and Ana were back in the kitchen, discussing which wall would come down, as well as drywall options—something Jacques specializes in.

In the living room, surrounded by the young couple's closest friends, *ma belle-sœur* Cécile and I helped ourselves to Ana's *quiche maison*. There were no chairs, and the only furniture was a fold-out plastic table where the buffet, including *une tarte aux pommes*, several boxed pizzas, and some homemade bread, was set. Noticing a few small gifts on the table, I wished I'd brought more than bread and toilet paper (*le PQ* seemed like a good idea, given the lack of supplies this first night). But this was really only a *premier coup de clé*, just hours after *la signature chez le notaire*, and not an official *crémaillère*. There would be plenty of time to find just the right *cadeau*—perhaps a lovely *tapis* to soften all the echoing. For now, though, it was enough to stand in this new space, surrounded by family, friends, the scent of homemade pie in the air, and the clickety-clack of dogs' paws marking their approval as little Izzy the beagle and Loca the French bulldog/Jack Russell bounded through the apartment.

Toasting to Max and Ana's new beginning, it felt magical how a simple set of keys could unlock so much more than a door. It had opened a new chapter—a place for laughter, shared meals, and the dreams these two *tourtereaux* continue to build together in their new nest between the sea and still-blossoming hills above.

FRENCH VOCABULARY

la crémaillère
housewarming party

la Route des Crêtes
"road across the crests"

la bruyère
heather

la fenêtre
window

la chambre d'amis
guest room

le pin parasol
umbrella pine

l'oursin (m)
sea urchin

la calanque
deep, rocky inlet

le déménagement
the house move

même pas peur
not even scared
(a playful or defiant expression to show bravery)

Je vais attaquer le papier peint
I'm going to tackle the wallpaper

le/la voisin(e)
neighbor

le rez-de-chaussée
ground floor

un aller-retour
round trip

la belle-soeur
sister-in-law
(also: step-sister)

la quiche maison
homemade quiche

la tarte aux pommes
apple tart

le PQ (papier toilette)
toilet paper

le premier coup de clé
first turn of the key

la signature chez le notaire
the signing at the notary's office

le cadeau
gift

le tapis
rug

DECEMBER

Decembre

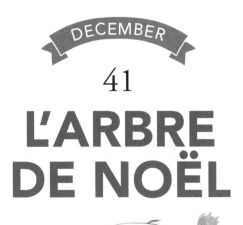

41

L'ARBRE
DE NOËL

On our way to walk Ricci on the beach, I paused at our neighborhood library—an old, beat-up telephone booth with its own certain charm—to check out the latest arrivals. There, perched atop a heap of books, was a familiar cover: *Almanach Provençal 2008*. I'd bought a copy years ago for its delightful watercolors and snippets of French customs, and here it was again, like an old friend rediscovered.

Entering the crowded *cabine téléphonique*, I picked up the book and opened it, eager to learn a few cultural insights for the French holidays. Flipping to the first week of December, a whimsical watercolor of an unusual Christmas tree caught my eye. The caption read: "…the beautiful potted olive tree is brought inside to become this year's Provençal Christmas tree…"

Studying the illustration of the *arbre de Noël*, with its simple, delicate embellishments, I was instantly charmed. The olive tree, with its bowl-like shape, slender trunk, and blue-green branches, was more than endearing—it was rich with meaning…

The Christmas tree hasn't always been a fir. In the Mediterranean, people once decorated olive trees for the holidays. With its evergreen leaves, the olive tree evokes Christ's entry into Jerusalem, and the nearby Mount of Olives. Its branches, a universal symbol of peace, make it a deeply meaningful choice for Christmas.

Tiens! L'olivier! What a refreshing change from the usual. And to my relief, there'd be no need to climb a ladder to fetch our artificial tree from storage. No more wrestling with wiry branches that needed unfurling or debating over who would help decorate this year.

With Max away in Montreal for his work in the wine business, Jackie leaving school and at a crossroads once again, and Jean-Marc preparing for his next adventure—soon to be making wine in Argentina—no one was around to assist. But the exotic simplicity of an olive tree felt like decoration enough. I could already picture it: a few ornaments, warm white lights, a crisp ribbon around the trunk, and a golden star to crown this uncelebrated savior of a Christmas tree.

Ça y est! This year's tree was practically chosen. All we needed now was to find it.

At our local *pépinière*, a young autistic man was carefully watering some poinsettias—*les étoiles de Noël* ("Christmas stars" in French). "Can you help us with an *olivier?*" I asked. "Oh, I don't know," he said, growing nervous. After some encouragement, he led us past rows of scentless *sapins*, through a back door, and paused at a quiet corner. There, we saw three types of olive trees: tiny potted ones (which I imagined disappearing behind a pile of wrapped presents), tall scraggly ones (too sparse for ornaments), and, finally, a last possibility—ornamental trees, similar to bonsais but much taller. They had a tall price tag, too!

One in particular stood out. Among all its neatly sculpted *rameaux*, one branch was bent back awkwardly toward the center. "*Merci!*" I said. "*Je vais réfléchir.*" But I had already made up my mind—this perfectly imperfect tree was *parfait* for our family. And, with a bit of girl math, I could almost justify the cost of this exotic olive tree *taillé en nuage*.

"Yes, thank you very much. You've been a great help," Jean-Marc added. Only then did the young man return to his watering, standing a little taller, his confidence visibly blooming.

Another man came over to help carry the olive tree to our Jimny. Hearing his southern French accent, I asked, "Do you know about the tradition of using olive trees as *sapins de Noël?*"

He grinned, tilting his head. "*Ah, mais oui! C'était d'avant, ça—*before we started importing Christmas trees…and Coca-Cola." His voice carried that unmistakable Provençal rhythm, the words rolling out like a song.

It took one more colleague to help lift the olive tree into the back of our little jeep, with Jean-Marc and me pulling vigorously from the front. But our efforts were halted when the tree got stuck halfway in. Just when it seemed we would break those cloud-shaped branches with our forcing…*whoosh!*…our leafy prize finally slid all the way in. There wasn't much room left in the passenger seat, but I managed to scooch in among the fragrant branches for the short ride back.

Once home, Jean-Marc and I lugged the tree into the house. With a bit of teamwork and loads of enthusiasm, we set it above the buffet. I loved seeing my husband fuss with its positioning, a small gesture that reassured me he valued the tree as much as I did, even though it might have seemed like a spontaneous buy. Quietly, we stepped back to admire this year's *arbre de Noël*. It was taller than expected, its leafy branches brushing the iron beam above. And, like so many of our previous Christmas trees, it was lopsided. But that didn't matter—I couldn't wait to show it off to Mom, our resident art director.

"It's fabulous!" Jules said, *époustouflée*. "You must keep it here year-round!"

When I shared the *pépinière's* warning that the olive tree wouldn't survive inside, Mom wasn't fazed. "After Christmas, you can put it in the garden and bring it in on weekends. Too bad it wasn't here for your dinner party last night! Why don't you invite everybody back?"

Just when I began fretting about more guests, Mom diffused any hostessing angst by changing the topic. "What will you name it?" she inquired. This got me smiling, for while I had resorted to using girl math to justify its purchase, Mom was already a step ahead, *making our olive tree priceless by adopting it.*

"*Voyons voir....* Let's see.... How about *Olivier*? It's French for olive tree."

"Ollie it is!" Mom declared, baptizing the newest member of our family. Like the rest of us, Ollie would soon be gussied up in a sparkly something, ready to put on her best for the upcoming *souper de Noël.*

That reminds me…one more tradition the Provençal Almanach mentions is *la pompe à l'huile*, the olive oil cake—Ollie's favorite dessert, I'm guessing. It's one of the *Treize Desserts* of a Provençal Christmas, symbolizing Christ and the Apostles. After all this time, you'd think I'd know more about that, but I have never settled down enough to grasp its meaning. *Comme quoi, il n'est jamais trop tard.* Perhaps I'll start by making one this year—and leave the *Apôtres* for later….

FRENCH VOCABULARY

L'arbre de Noël (m)
Christmas tree

l'almanach provençal (m)
Provençal almanac

la cabine téléphonique
telephone booth

Tiens! L'olivier
Hey! The olive tree!

Ça y est
that's it!

la pépinière
nursery

les étoiles (f) de Noël
Christmas stars, poinsettias

le sapin
fir tree

le rameau
branch

merci
thank you

je vais réfléchir
I'm going to think about it

parfait
perfect

la taille en nuage
cloud pruning

le sapin de Noël
Christmas tree

Ah, mais oui!
yes, of course

C'était d'avant, ça
that was from olden days

époustouflé(e)
amazed

voyons voir
let's see

le souper de Noël
Christmas dinner

la pompe à l'huile
olive oil cake

les Treize Desserts (m)
Thirteen Desserts

Comme quoi, il n'est jamais trop tard
That goes to show, it's never too late

l'Apôtre (m)
the Apostle

42
LA POMPE
À L'HUILE

*I*f I learned French from books and teachers, and if it was my French family and friends who grew and tended my vocabulary, would you believe it was a humble cake that taught me *la Cène*?

The discovery came while I was leafing through *l'Almanach Provençal*, a treasure trove of Provençal traditions. I had just admired a sweetly decorated olive tree when my gaze landed on another ancient Christmas custom: *la Pompe à l'Huile*.

My first encounter with this *gâteau* was years ago at Cousin Sabine's. Married to Jean-Marc's cousin François, Sabine often hosts *Le Gros Souper* at their family vineyard nestled in the fragrant foothills of *la montagne Sainte-Victoire*. It was there I first discovered *les santons* and their bustling village scenes: little clay figurines representing the local characters of Provence—*la boulangère*, *le chasseur*, and *l'homme ravi*, among others.

Sabine's *crèche* was an elaborate tableau, complete with fresh moss gathered from the surrounding hills to form the floor of a miniature Provençal village. Off to the side but at the heart of it all was *l'étable*, the humble stable, quietly anchoring the scene.

After admiring the nativity scene, we gathered around Sabine's mile-long dining table to enjoy a traditional feast that lasted until the sun dipped below the horizon. Annie, Sabine's mom, served home-grown chickpeas, still warm from the *cocotte-minute*. Sabine's father, André, a hunter, tended the wild *faisan* which cooked in the fireplace beside our festive meal. A host of other dishes circulated the grand table along with family wines including Uncle Jean-Claude's *Domaine du Banneret*, from Châteauneuf-du-Pape. Then came the grand finale: the thirteen desserts, each laden with symbolism, representing Jesus Christ and the Twelve Apostles.

Among the sweets, I'll never forget *la pompe à l'huile*. Modest and unadorned, these characteristics remind me of the manger, where Christ lay as a newborn. No matter how many times we sang *Away in a Manger* growing up, for me, it took learning French to fully grasp the poignancy of the English word "manger" in this exact context: Our Lord was laid in none other than a *feeding trough for animals*.

As for the *pompe à l'huile*, there was nothing pompous about its appearance. No icing, no layers, no filling—not even a *couronne*, like the one sported by another popular (but equally plain) cake. No, this *pompe à l'huile* was as plain as a felled *sapin*: a simple, round loaf delicately scented with orange blossom water and made with olive oil—its namesake. Its history may explain its rustic charm. Born of necessity, the dessert originated as a way to save the last precious drops of oil from the press. Flour was used to "pump" or absorb the oil, with a touch of sugar added…and *voilà*! The flat cake was born, evolving over generations into the humble yet symbolic *spécialité* served in Provence during the holidays.

I remember Sabine offering me a slice. I was hesitant. Olive oil? In a cake? It seemed counterintuitive—like eating dessert with spoons, as my tablemates were doing. But as I took a bite, something magical happened. Perhaps it was Sabine's smile or the warm hospitality that transformed my palate. By the time my tastebuds registered, I could honestly answer her question.

"*Alors?*" Sabine asked in her Provençal accent. "*Tu aimes?*"

"Yes. I love it!"

Years passed, and though I loved the cake, I never attempted to make it. Part of me believed only a dyed-in-the-wool Provençal woman could do justice to such a traditional recipe. But this week, curiosity (and courage) got the better of me.

I lined up the ingredients: olive oil, water, egg, grated orange peel, flour, sugar, salt, *fleur d'oranger*, and *levain*. After mixing the ingredients, I shaped the dough on a lined baking sheet, scoring decorative lines across the top with a knife. Into the oven it went (350°F…20-25 minutes).

When the timer chimed, I opened the oven door, and a whoosh of warm, citrus-scented air enveloped me. There it was—a golden cake, its surface glistening faintly. Despite a few miscalculations, *c'était réussi*! But what about *la Cène*? For years, I had taken bread and wine (that is, grape juice) at church without fully understanding the meaning of this French term for the Last Supper. Each time the pastor said the word, I wondered: was it *la Seine*—the river in Paris? Or perhaps *la saine* (the healthy one)? Then again, could it be *la scène* (the stage)? I thought our visiting pastor might finally clear up the mystery, but his thick Scottish accent while speaking

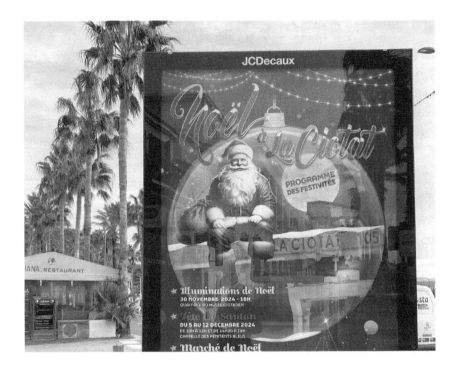

French only added to the kaleidoscope of possibilities for what this word could mean. *Sin? Seen? Sane?*

My confusion lingered until this week, when I stumbled upon *la Pompe à l'Huile* while researching the thirteen desserts of Noël. That's when I came across the spelling of this word I had heard so often in church—*la Cène*. Suddenly, everything clicked: it was the Last Supper of Christ and His apostles!

How fitting that a humble cake, steeped in tradition, would finally unravel the mystery for me.

Don't wait as long as I did to learn the meaning of certain French words, especially *la Cène*. And don't delay in trying this modest cake—it's a lesson in simplicity, an authentic taste of Provence, and a slice of history all in one. *Joyeuses Fêtes!*

SIMPLE RECIPE FOR
LA POMPE À L'HUILE

INGREDIENTS:

250g (2 cups) all-purpose flour

75g (⅓ cup) sugar

¼ tsp salt

1 tsp baking powder

60ml (¼ cup) olive oil (preferably extra virgin)

60ml (¼ cup) orange blossom water

Zest of 1 orange

1 egg

¼ cup warm water

INSTRUCTIONS:

Preheat oven to 180°C (350°F). Line a baking sheet with parchment paper.

Mix the dry ingredients: In a large bowl, combine the flour, sugar, salt, and baking powder.

Prepare the wet ingredients: In a separate bowl, whisk together the olive oil, orange blossom water, orange zest, egg, and warm water.

Combine the wet and dry ingredients: Gradually pour the wet mixture into the dry ingredients, stirring with a spoon until a soft dough forms.

Shape the dough: Place the dough onto the prepared baking sheet and gently press it into a round, flat shape about 1.5 cm (1/2 inch) thick. Use a rolling pin if necessary. Use a knife to make a few decorative slashes across the surface.

Bake: Bake for 20-25 minutes or until the edges are lightly golden. Let cool slightly before serving.

FRENCH VOCABULARY

la pompe à l'huile
traditional Provençal
olive oil cake

La Cène
The Last Supper

**l'Almanach
Provençal (m)**
the Provençal
Almanac

Le Gros Souper (m)
The Big Supper
(for Christmas)

**la montagne
Sainte-Victoire**
Sainte-Victoire
mountain

les santons (m)
traditional Provençal
clay figurines

la boulangère
the baker

le chasseur
the hunter

l'homme ravi (m)
the delighted man

la crèche
nativity scene

l'étable (f)
stable, barn

la cocotte-minute
pressure cooker

le faisan
pheasant, game bird

la couronne
crown

le sapin
Christmas tree

voilà!
presto!

la spécialité
specialty

alors?
well?

tu aimes?
do you like it?

fleur d'oranger
orange blossom

le levain
leaven, sourdough
starter

c'était réussi
it was a success

La Seine
river in Paris

saine
healthy

la scène
the stage

Joyeuses Fêtes!
Merry Christmas!
Happy Holidays!

43

C'EST LE GESTE QUI COMPTE

*E*ntering the studio on the side of our house, I find Mom bundled in bed, laptop propped on a pillow, watching the exciting *réouverture de Notre-Dame* in Paris. Organ music fills the room, and the iconic *église*, now rebuilt after the devastating fire five and a half years ago, sparkles brightly from Jules's side. But no matter how glorious the event on the screen, Mom will shut it off to give her full attention to her visitor.

Since our golden retriever Smokey passed away, and 20-year-old Lili the cat moved back to the neighbor's (unwilling to share the yard with Ricci), Mom's ever-present companion has become her laptop. Connected to the speaker Max gave her, for better sound, Jules's computer has become her portal to limitless adventures. With a single click, she's back with her neighborhood horses in a barrio in Mexico, tending stray dogs in Greece, or soaring over France's beloved cathedral for a view far better than even the president's!

Sliding shut the front door, I set down my keys and phone and join Mom in her world, sharing her excitement or concern, depending on the news she's watching. However different our views on politics and current events may be at times, we try not to get too caught up in these passing emotions. *Peu importe*, the two of us always seem to find a truce over food.

"I've made another *pompe à l'huile*," I say, grinning. "Version number three. Want to try it?"

"That sounds good! You go ahead, Honey. I'll be right over."

I head back, with Ricci trotting close behind. High up on a branch of our bay laurel tree, resident doves Mama and Papa follow our every move. Moments later, Mom arrives with two polished apples, *les Reines des Reinettes* ("Queen of Queens"). She places them on our coffee table as if part of a still life. When invited over for a snack or a meal, Jules's automatic response is reciprocity: her spontaneous gifts range from canned peppers to sautéed shrimp to ice cream cones. Offer Mom flowers in a tall glass vase, and she'll divide the bouquet in two, creating an elaborate *tableau vivant*—a living picture—by arranging the second half artfully in a clay bowl for my coffee table.

It's a lovely reminder of a timeless custom and a simple truth: *il ne faut jamais arriver les mains vides* (never arrive empty-handed).

While we're here, and before we return to our narrative, here are a few more thoughts in French concerning gift-giving:

- *C'est le geste qui compte.*
- *Donner, c'est mieux que recevoir.*
- *Le cadeau n'est rien, c'est l'intention qui compte.*

"Your tree looks beautiful with the lights," Mom says, entering through the sliding glass door, taking Ricci into her lap after settling on the couch.

"Do you think I should add ornaments? I've got blue stars and reindeer…"

"I would leave it just as it is!"

"I like that idea!"

Presently, *les santons*—what clay figurines we have left—are crowded at the base of the olive tree. After Jean-Marc borrowed *la crèche* for his wine shop a few years back, a few characters disappeared. A quick inventory reveals we still have *le porteur d'eau, la bergère, les rois mages*—and Joseph—but no sign of Mary, and, good lord, Jesus has gone missing! But there's time to find him (yes, it's never too late to find Jesus!).

"What do you want for your birthday?" Mom changes the subject.

"You already got me something: I've ordered the fluffy wool faux fur *coussin* for my writing chair."

"Good! Now let's get you something else!"

I stop to revel in Mom's generosity when suddenly she asks, "How old will you be?"

"57."

"57! You should have a present every day!"

"Aw, Mom. What about you? What would you like for Christmas?"

"Pajamas. *I want my whole wardrobe to be pajamas!*"

I laugh and hug her, a warm, unspoken understanding passing between us. No matter our ups and downs this past year, Mom will always be the apple of my eye, the queen of queens—just like those polished Reinettes she brought me.

It's these little moments—the laughter, the shared joy—that are the gifts that keep on giving. Whether for Christmas, birthdays, or any day, time with a loved one is the most precious *cadeau* of all.

FRENCH VOCABULARY

**c'est le geste
qui compte**
it's the thought
that counts

la réouverture
the reopening

Notre-Dame (f)
[literally,
"Our Lady"]
cathedral in Paris

l'église (f)
church

peu importe
no matter what

la pompe à l'huile
traditional
olive oil bread

**la Reine
des Reinettes**
Queen of Queens
(type of apple)

le tableau vivant
living picture

**il ne faut
jamais arriver
les mains vides**
never arrive
empty-handed

**donner, c'est
mieux que recevoir**
it is better to give
than to receive

**le cadeau
n'est rien,
c'est l'intention
qui compte**
the gift is nothing;
it's the intention
that counts

le santon
figurine from
a Provençal
nativity scene

le porteur d'eau
water carrier

la bergère
shepherdess

les rois mages
the three wise men

le coussin
cushion

le cadeau
gift

DECEMBER

44

LA RECONNAISSANCE

*C*nd just like that, 2024 has come to an end. As they say here in Provence, *Bon bout d'an!*—happy end of the year.

How quickly the months have gone by. Like the gentle breeze sweeping the neighborhood leaves across the seafront, *le temps vole!* But to where, exactly, does time fly? However boggling this vast endlessness, there's comfort in knowing these moments live on forever, in our memories, in our stories, and even into the mysterious ever after.

Looking back over the past four seasons, I'm filled with gratitude and *émerveillement*—not only for the unexpected people who came into our lives but for those who've been there all along, making every little adventure and its built-in lesson more precious, meaningful, and lasting.

The year began with an intention to connect more deeply with the locals. I imagined myself frequenting cafés, supporting local establishments, and finding ways to weave more threads into the vibrant tapestry of life here in La Ciotat. But the universe had other plans. Instead of reaching out to others, it seemed others were sent to me, offering help in ways I couldn't have anticipated.

The first spark came early in the year, on a sunny day at the farmer's market. I had tied Ricci's leash to a table while picking out some fresh vegetables. I turned away for just a moment, and when I looked back, she was gone.

In a panic, I rushed down the boardwalk, calling her name. But before I could begin to lose hope, several locals sprang into action, hurrying ahead to corral Ricci and guide her back to me. One after another, they closed the gaps, gently steering her back into my arms. That day, I realized just how quickly people can step in to help when you least expect it—and how much I relied on the kindness of strangers which appears when we least expect it.

When my husband left for New Zealand, my confidence in steering this boat quickly dwindled with the arrival of the first obstacles. Mom's health began to require more attention, and with a medical appointment looming, I realized I would have to dust off my driving skills after years of being Jean-Marc's passenger.

But I wasn't alone. Ana, Max's girlfriend, immediately offered to chauffeur us to the *ophtalmologue* and Jackie chaperoned us to the next appointment. Watching these young women navigate so calmly reminded me how much we all lean on each other, no matter our inner strength. As I slowly regained my confidence behind the wheel, what began as an ordeal opened a path for me to reclaim a bit of independence.

The challenges continued when we discovered Mom's health card had expired. I braced myself for a bureaucratic nightmare, unsure how we'd navigate the French healthcare system. But once again, help came in the form of angels—nurses, hospital staff, and administrative workers—who quietly and compassionately ensured Mom received the care she needed, regardless of the expired paperwork.

In the end, all her bills were covered, a testament to the grace of a system and the people within it who prioritize compassion over red tape. I was deeply humbled by their quiet *bienveillance*.

Any challenges this year were punctuated by joys. In February, raising a glass of *eau pétillante*, I toasted to 21 cherished years of sobriety. In July, Jean-Marc and I celebrated our 30th anniversary and in October my dad, sisters, and I reunited on a Mediterranean cruise! You know it's been a good year when you get to dig out your wedding dress and wear it twice (once for our anniversary dinner and again for the cruise's White Night party).

In the fall, the tables turned, and I experienced an unexpected health issue. Physical therapy and the support of friends and family got me through. This year, I meant to reach out to others, but instead, they reached out to me. From locals at the market, to loved ones, and the medical angels who showed up when we needed them most, I was reminded again and again of the quiet ways grace flows into our lives.

Recalling everyone who played a part in this period of our lives, I owe so much to my readers. Thank you for helping me realize my goal of writing another year of stories. To those who followed my blog, commented, emailed, and encouraged me—you may not know it, but your support kept me showing up at the blank page, typing away. Writing isn't something I can do in isolation. A weekly deadline in which I report to you from here provides just enough pressure to "gather all the butterflies"—or happenings— and settle them into a meaningful essay. I'm learning to live with the anxiety, though I sometimes think, *Why not just settle down in the garden and let the butterflies be?* Wouldn't that be more relaxing?

I do not know what drives me to write, but your presence gives me the motivation to keep sharing.

Special thanks to my book angels at TLC Book Design: Tami Dever, for taking on this book project and helping to market it, to Erin Stark, for designing the beautiful interior and for all her detailed work, thoughts, prayers, and valuable time, and to Monica Thomas, for the wonderful series of book covers she created so that readers could pick the winner!

Mille mercis from the heart to my dedicated proofreaders Agnès Gros, Rajeev Bansal, Liz Caughey, and Sara Rubin—thank you for your invaluable feedback, edits, and precious time spent correcting this manuscript. To Chief Grape, chief of my heart, Jean-Marc, to Mom, and to my family, near and far, thank you for your love and patience. And to my longtime bestie, Susan Boehnstedt, a.k.a.

Rouge-Bleu, for your timely WhatsApp check-ins—a needed diversion from the daily act of juggling life.

One year ago, I never imagined the quartet of helpers who would come into our home: *un grand merci* to the nurses, Nathalie, Roland, and Nicolas, and to our *fée du logis*, Fiona, who is like a daughter. Finally, thanks to my *frères et sœurs* at Église Évangélique Baptiste. France will always be a foreign land, but this little church feels as familiar as home.

As I sit here, watching the waves roll in along the shore in La Ciotat, I am overwhelmed by *reconnaissance*. These past twelve months weren't what I imagined, but they taught me to open my heart and receive the help of others.

The phrase I mentioned earlier, *bon bout d'an*, is often followed by another: *et à l'an que ven*—"and to the coming year." I leave you with many cheers and hope the new year finds you open-hearted, and ready to receive countless blessings. When you get the chance, lie in a garden and wait quietly for the butterflies or angels—*grace* in whichever form it may appear.

FRENCH VOCABULARY

la reconnaissance
acknowledgment,
gratefulness

Bon bout d'an
Happy end
of the year

le temps vole
time flies

**l'émerveillement
(m)**
awe

**l'ophtalmologue,
l'ophtalmologiste**
opthlamologist

la bienveillance
kindness, goodwill

l'eau pétillante (f)
sparkling water

mille mercis
a thousand thanks

un grand merci
a big thank-you

la fée du logis
house helper

mes frères et sœurs
my brothers
and sisters

**bon bout d'an
et à l'an que ven**
Provençal for
"happy end of the
year and to the
coming year"

ABOUT THE AUTHOR

Kristin Ingham Espinasse was born in 1967 in Angeles City, Philippines, where her father was stationed with the U.S. Air Force. Raised by her mother in Phoenix, Arizona, Kristi developed a love for French culture, earning a BA in French from Arizona State University in 1991 and graduating cum laude. After meeting her husband, French winemaker Jean-Marc Espinasse, in Aix-en-Provence, she moved to France in 1994.

The couple lived on two vineyards and in several picturesque towns, including Marseille, St.-Maximin, Les Arcs-sur-Argens, Sainte-Cécile-les-Vignes, St.-Cyr-sur-Mer, before settling in La Ciotat. Their children, Max (born in 1995) and Jackie (born in 1997), were raised in the vibrant culture of southern France.

In 2002, Kristi launched her blog, French-Word-A-Day (French-Word-a-Day.com), a beloved resource for Francophiles. A passionate photographer, she captures the charm of French towns and landscapes. Kristi also writes the column "Le Dernier Mot" for France Today Magazine. In 2021, she was awarded La Médaille d'Or des Valeurs Francophones for her support of French language and culture by La Renaissance Française.

PHOTO: SUSAN BOEHNSTEDT

These stories continue
at French-Word-a-Day.com

Made in the USA
Las Vegas, NV
21 March 2025

19843065R00174